BEER QUEST WEST

THE CRAFT BREWERS OF ALBERTA AND BRITISH COLUMBIA

JON C. STOTT

TouchWood
Editions

TouchWood Editions
www.touchwoodeditions.com

LIBRARY AND ARCHIVES CANADA CATALOGUING IN PUBLICATION
Stott, Jon C., date
Beer quest west : the craft brewers of Alberta and British Columbia / Jon C. Stott.

Includes index.
Print format: ISBN 978-1-926741-16-1
Electronic monograph in PDF format: ISBN 978-1-926741-32-1
Electronic monograph in HTML format: ISBN 978-1-926741-33-8

1. Microbreweries—Alberta—Guidebooks. 2. Microbreweries—British Columbia—
Guidebooks. 3. Breweries--Alberta—Guidebooks. 4. Breweries—British Columbia—
Guidebooks. 5. Beer—Alberta. 6. Beer—British Columbia. I. Title.

TP573.C3S76 2011   663'.4209711   C2010-907379-7

Editor: Marlyn Horsdal
Proofreader: Holland Gidney
Design: Pete Kohut
Cover image: Patricia Hofmeester, istockphoto.com
All interior photos by the author unless otherwise credited.

We gratefully acknowledge the financial support for our publishing activities
from the Government of Canada through the Canada Book Fund, Canada
Council for the Arts, and the province of British Columbia through the
British Columbia Arts Council and the Book Publishing Tax Credit.

MIX
Paper from
responsible sources
FSC® C016245

The interior pages of this book have been printed on 100% post-consumer
recycled paper, processed chlorine free, and printed with vegetable-based inks.

The information in this book is true and complete to the best of the author's knowledge.
All recommendations are made without guarantee on the part of the author. The author
disclaims any liability in connection with the use of this information.

1 2 3 4 5 14 13 12 11

PRINTED IN CANADA

Dedicated to John Mitchell, Frank Appleton, Paul Hadfield, Mitch Taylor, and Ed McNally, who introduced Albertans and British Columbians to really good beer.

Things change, people move, and we don't want you to miss anything! Check online for *Beer Quest West* updates and news at beerquestwest.com.

Contents

After "Beer"

Before the middle of the 1980s, I drank "beer." Until the late 1970s, it was Molson Canadian, because it sponsored *Hockey Night in Canada*. But when the Montreal Canadiens, then owned by Molson, voted against accepting the Edmonton Oilers into the National Hockey League, I joined a Molson boycott and switched to Labatt Blue. When I visited the United States, I drank Budweiser. But regardless of who brewed it, I thought of it merely as "beer." It was pretty much the same, no matter what label was on the bottle—pale, highly carbonated, and bland. Occasionally, I'd show my multiculturalism by ordering Tsingtao (which was really a German-style lager) when we went out for Chinese food or would demonstrate my sophistication by sipping Heineken when we went to an expensive steak house. But usually it was just "beer." It was cheaper than European imports and, if you drank a few bottles, you'd have profound thoughts about politics, sports, and sex to share with the nearest unwilling listener.

In 1986, I discovered there was more than "beer." One night at the fancy steak house, the waiter suggested that I try Traditional Ale, something new from Calgary. He said it was different, something called an English dark mild. It didn't look like "beer"—it was so dark you could hardly see through it. And it didn't taste like "beer"—in fact it had taste. Then, a few weeks later, during a visit to Victoria, friends took us to Spinnakers. "The place has a great view of the water, and they have a little brewery." I chose something called Extra Special Bitter, not because I knew what that was, but because I remembered my father saying that he'd had it during a vacation in England. It wasn't really bitter, but it did taste different, not only from "beer" but from Traditional Ale. But, like Traditional, it tasted good. A few months later, while I was attending a conference in the United States, a waiter invited me to try a product that they'd just begun to carry: Sierra Nevada Pale Ale. It didn't look pale, more a deep gold or amber. It had a not-unpleasant bitterness, a taste different from anything I'd experienced before.

I didn't realize until many years later that my 1986 experiences had occurred in the earlier years of what would be sometimes called the Microbrewing Revolution—a movement in which small breweries would recreate old styles of ales and lagers that had been almost completely replaced in the preceding half century by "beer." Over the next decade, I still drank "beer," but more and more, I found myself looking, at home and during my travels, for microbrewery products. Soon I discovered that Alberta and British Columbia brewers were starting to make some really fine ales and lagers, many of which I could find in liquor stores in Edmonton. I didn't stick to one brand or one style as I had when I drank "beer." It was fun to discover new styles and to compare the same styles produced by different microbreweries. By the beginning of this century, the only time I would have "beer," one of the products of the giant breweries, was when I was visiting a beer-benighted friend and was too polite to say no to what he offered.

The idea for writing a book about the thriving microbrewing scene in Alberta and British Columbia came to me on a snowy evening late in October 2008. That afternoon, I'd visited Edmonton's Sherbrooke Liquor Store, where, after looking at the dozens of different kinds of ales and lager in the cold room, I bought a six-pack of Pumpkin Pi, a seasonal brew from Edmonton's Alley Kat Brewing Company.

Back home, I poured a glass, settled in front of the fireplace to sip, and began reading *Driving to Detroit: an Automotive Odyssey*, sent to me by a friend who knew my love of themed travel books. It was the account of a circuitous journey made by Lesley Hazleton, automotive writer for the *Seattle Times*, from her Washington State home to the Detroit Automotive Show. After I'd finished the first chapter and my glass of Pumpkin Pi—a really delicious beer in which the pumpkin and spice notes didn't overwhelm the malt and hop flavours—I began to think that it would be fun to travel through Alberta and BC, visiting microbreweries and brewpubs in the two provinces, talking with owners and brewers about the more than two hundred varieties of beer they brewed, sampling (after each day's driving and visiting, and when I'd returned home) as many of these as possible, and then writing about what I'd learned, experienced, and tasted.

When I suggested the idea to Pat Touchie and Ruth Linka of TouchWood Editions, they responded enthusiastically. We agreed that such a book would include brief historical contexts about brewing in the two provinces, as well as in the Yukon, with an emphasis on the growth of microbreweries since the 1980s, and brief descriptions of the brewing process and brewing styles. The focus of the book would be on the breweries I visited during my "quest." After presenting the background of each brewery, I'd profile the owners and brewers and then discuss their beers, using, as much as possible, the brewers' own words to describe their creations. I would not provide ratings or personal evaluations of individual beers because responses to the same beer can vary greatly from individual to individual, depending on palate, preference, and personal beer history. I would write only about those breweries where the entire brewing process was carried out on the premises, excluding the three or four places that use wort that is prepared elsewhere and delivered to them, and then merely add yeast to begin the fermentation process.

Over the next several months, I read many of the growing number of books about the history and making of beer and about the tremendous variety of styles created by the growing number of microbreweries in Canada and the United States. I also made several trips to the Sherbrooke Liquor Store, bringing home BC, Alberta, and Yukon beers. I began my travels in the summer of 2009, with visits to Alberta breweries, continued in the fall and winter with trips through the BC Interior and to the Lower Mainland, and concluded in the spring of 2010 with a visit to Vancouver Island. My travels ended at Spinnakers in Victoria. I was able to visit all but four of the microbreweries in my area of interest. With three of these—Pacific Western, Plan B, and Yukon—I conducted telephone interviews. Two new brewpubs, The Moon Under Water, in Victoria, and The Noble Pig Brewhouse, in Kamloops, opened too late to be included in this book. Unfortunately, several attempts to arrange either an in-person brewery visit or a telephone interview with staff at Turning Point Brewery were unsuccessful. *Beer Quest West* presents the record of what I learned in my reading, travelling, interviewing, and tasting. Each chapter presents the breweries and brewpubs in a geographical area, and my discussions of the individual operations are arranged in the order in which I visited them.

Although the glossary and the appendix on beer styles are intended to provide readers with definitions of the beer terms found throughout the book, four are used so frequently that they should be defined here:

Lager: one of the two main categories of beer. Lagers use bottom-fermenting yeasts, take longer to brew, and are fermented at lower temperatures. Generally, they are lighter in colour and body than ales. Most of the beer drunk around the world is North American lager, a style best exemplified by Budweiser.

Ale: the other main category of beer. Ales use top-fermenting yeasts, take less time to brew, and are fermented at higher temperatures. They are generally darker in colour and more full-bodied and robustly flavoured than lagers.

Microbrewery: a term used to describe breweries that have an annual production of less than twenty thousand hectolitres in Alberta and less than sixty thousand in BC. Nearly all of the breweries discussed in this book are microbreweries, although some, such as Granville Island and Big Rock, have become very large and are often called regional breweries.

Alcohol by Volume, ABV: The percentage of alcohol in beer is measured either by weight or by volume. As measuring alcohol by volume is most common, it is the unit used in this book.

This book could not have been written without the great help of many people. I wish first to thank Pat and Rodger Touchie and Ruth Linka for encouraging me to undertake the project and for supporting me throughout the research and writing. Thank you also to Marlyn Horsdal for much-appreciated editorial guidance. I want to thank the more than one hundred owners and brewers with whom I talked before, during, and after my travels. These people gave graciously of their time, answering my countless questions and patiently explaining the art of creating beer and the business of selling it. They thoughtfully restricted my on-site tasting of their beers and generously gave me samples to take home. Finally, to the five men whose names appear on the dedication page go my thanks, along with the thanks of thousands of craft-beer drinkers. Without their pioneering efforts, the beer scene in western Canada would still be about "beer."

Beginnings
1984 and Ale That

In 1980, ten breweries operated in Alberta, British Columbia, and the Yukon. Molson had plants in Edmonton, Lethbridge, and Vancouver; Carling-O'Keefe in Calgary and Vancouver; and Labatt in Edmonton, Creston, New Westminster, and Victoria There was one independent brewery in Prince George. Three decades later, only four of these breweries still existed: Labatt's Edmonton and Creston operations, Molson's Vancouver plant, and the Prince George brewery, now known as Pacific Western. The 1989 merger of Molson and Carling-O'Keefe and the introduction of laws permitting the major brewers to transport their product across provincial borders had led to the closing of six plants.

However, by the middle of 2010, the total number of breweries in the three areas had risen to seventy-three, including thirty-one brewpubs, three combined brewpubs-microbreweries, and thirty-six microbreweries. While Labatt and Molson Coors still produced mainly pale, North American-style lagers, these brewpubs and microbreweries brewed an amazing variety of styles, ranging from Czech pilsners and English pale ales to Irish stouts and Belgian *lambics*.

The growth in the number of these smaller breweries was part of a trend in Canada and the United States that had its beginnings in the late 1970s and early 1980s. Some of the influences came from outside Canada. In England, a group known as the Campaign for Real Ale (CAMRA) objected to the fact that most English pubs were controlled by large breweries that served mainly a variety of the pale lagers so popular in the US. CAMRA encouraged a return to the brewing of flavourful ales in the traditional ways. Along the US Pacific coast, many small new breweries developed new recipes for pale ales, generously hopping them with local varieties of the bittering ingredient so important to the style. People returning to Canada after visits to England or the US spoke enthusiastically about the wonderful "new beers" they had discovered and frequently brought home samples to share with their friends.

When he opened Horseshoe Bay Brewery in 1982, John Mitchell
began Canada's modern microbrewing movement.

It could be said facetiously that the microbrewing movement in
Canada began because of a BC beer strike, two magazine articles, and
a British expatriate's trip back home. John Mitchell, who had come to
Canada in 1954, was part owner of the Troller Pub in Horseshoe Bay
when, in 1979, the BC divisions of Canada's three major breweries went
on strike. "At first we had no beer; then we were allowed to bring in

American beer from Washington State. BC and the US beers were not very good: pale yellow, bland, fizzy swill that embodied the Myth of the Three Cs—that beer must be cold, clear, and carbonated," Mitchell recalled. He became particularly displeased with the products available for him to serve when he heard that Expo 86 had been granted to Vancouver. "All these people from around the world—and we wouldn't have any good Canadian beer to serve them," he lamented.

Just before Mitchell and his family returned to England for a summer vacation, he read an article in the *Illustrated London News* about London-area pubs that had begun brewing their own beer. He dropped in on some of them and discovered that they were creating beers as wonderful as the ones he remembered from his youth. He had just returned to Canada, even more dissatisfied with what he could serve the customers at Troller, when one of the regulars showed him a *Harrowsmith Reader Volume II* article that mourned the decline in flavour of Canadian beers during the three decades that the (then) three major Canadian breweries had been increasing their control of the Canadian beer industry. It went on to outline the steps of homebrewing and included recipes for a light lager, a medium ale, and an oatmeal stout. Mitchell was fascinated.

Frank Appleton, the author of the article, was a fellow Brit who had worked for a decade as a quality control supervisor at Carling-O'Keefe's Vancouver brewery before he resigned in disgust at what he considered the increasingly inferior qualities of beer that the major breweries were marketing. Years later, he recounted what happened the day after Mitchell read his article. "I lived in Edgewater, a small town in the Kootenays, writing and doing some homebrewing. One morning the phone rang and the caller identified himself as John Mitchell, one of the owners of a pub at Horseshoe Bay. We talked and he asked if he could pay me a visit. He and his wife, Jenny, arrived a couple of days later, loaded with food and some English beer he still had from a trip home." Over the next few days, Mitchell and Appleton developed a plan: they would submit a proposal for a brewpub—a type of business that didn't exist in Canada—to the BC government and, if it was accepted, Appleton would help Mitchell set up a small brewery and teach him to brew.

The two presented the proposal first to Alan Gould of the Liquor Control Board and then to Peter Hyndman, provincial minister of

Consumer and Corporate Affairs. Both supported the idea and subsequently, the Legislature passed a law making the brewpub idea a reality—if the brewery were located across a public road from the pub itself. When Horseshoe Bay Brewery and Troller Pub served their first beer, Bay Ale, in June 1982, Canada's first modern brewpub was opened.

Appleton cautioned Mitchell to begin with one beer, to make it well, and to get known. "I asked him to tell me about what kind of beer he'd liked and he told me Fuller's London Pride, an English bitter. We used this as the basis of our recipe and developed an English mild." Mitchell had told his business partners that the pub would need to sell one or two casks a day to break even. But they ran through eight the first night and were out of beer during the second week. As word quickly spread about the new beer, the small brewery, cobbled together out of used dairy equipment from Vancouver, was barely, and sometimes not, able to keep up with demand.

In 1983, a similar brewery/pub combination opened in Saanichton, north of Victoria. The Prairie Inn Neighbourhood Pub and Cottage Brewery were housed in adjacent buildings, one of which had been a tavern since 1859. They served malt extract beers and operated until the mid-1990s; the pub still exists.

Another trip John Mitchell made to England resulted in his becoming involved in a second historical event in Canadian brewing history, the creation of Victoria's Spinnakers, the country's first self-contained modern brewpub and, in 2010, its longest in continuous operation. Mitchell and a group of friends had gathered to share a suitcase of bottled beer he'd brought back from England. One of the members of the group was Paul Hadfield, a Victoria-born architect living in North Vancouver. "I remember we sat around tasting the different beers and talking about beer recipes," Hadfield recalled. Out of the gathering came the decision that Hadfield, Mitchell, and others would investigate opening a brewpub in Victoria.

"We really wanted something at the waterfront, because I'd heard that waterfront restaurants did very well. When I found this character home on the waterfront in Vic West, I was very excited." The south-facing waterfront property was not part of the trendy, upscale location it is today. Although it looked across the Strait of Juan de Fuca to the

Spinnakers Gastro Brewpub, Canada's longest
continuously operating brewpub, opened in 1984.

Olympic Mountains in Washington State, the site for this neighbourhood pub wasn't exactly in a neighbourhood. To the east were industrial
buildings and petroleum tanks, and to the west small, old houses. But
the late-nineteenth-century stone house that Hadfield wanted to convert
into the pub definitely had possibilities.

As had been the case for the Troller Pub operation, the partners had
to jump through several legal hoops—obstacles that, Hadfield surmised,
were encouraged by the major breweries protecting their territory in
Victoria. First, the city required a hearing with area residents about such
an establishment opening up in their neighbourhood. "We were called
a neighbourhood pub, although there wasn't really any neighbourhood
right around us. But the people in Vic West and Esquimalt were all very
supportive." Then the partners had to approach the federal government
for changes to the excise tax law, which prohibited products subject
to excise tax from being manufactured and sold in the same building.
Finally, when plans for the building were presented to Liquor Control

Board inspectors, they asked Hadfield about the number and placement of windows and the location of the stage on which the "dancers" would perform. The question about the windows was prompted by officials' fears that young passersby might be able to look in on the "dancers." Hadfield explained that the only thing customers might gaze intently at were views of sea, sailboats, and mountains, and that the windows were designed so that they could do so.

While Hadfield was dealing with legal details and answering questions about windows and dancers, John Mitchell and Frank Appleton were working on the practical aspects of getting the brewery up and running. Having learned the difficulties of working with an aging, piecemeal brewing system, they decided to order new, custom-made equipment, which is still operating, from an English company. They also, on Hadfield's recommendation, developed and tested recipes for three beers, each an English-style brew. Jenny Mitchell, who had run the kitchen at Troller Pub, worked on a pub-food menu that included, not surprisingly, fish and chips.

In the morning of Tuesday, May 15, 1984, the inspector from the Liquor Control Board dropped by for a final look around, and at 2:00 in the afternoon, Hadfield received a call asking him to come to the LCB offices to pick up the liquor licence. "People had been calling us all day," he remembered, "asking if we were going to open that day and at what time." Two hours later, he turned on the cash register and the sixty-five-seat brewpub was open. Mitchell and Appleton had been unable to brew their own beer commercially until the licence had been granted, but on the morning of May 16, they began production. A month later, on Saturday, June 16, they served their first beers: Spinnakers, a light-bodied golden ale, Saanichton ESB, and Mt. Tolmie Dark, an English mild. English expatriates were delighted to rediscover the styles they had enjoyed during their earlier beer-drinking years. Nobody asked where the dancers were.

In 1983, three short-lived microbreweries opened in BC: Mountain Ales in Surrey, Bryant's Brewery in Maple Ridge, and North Island Brewing in Campbell River. A year later, Granville Island Brewing Company opened in Vancouver and is now the oldest continuously operating microbrewery in Canada.

Granville Island Brewing Company, almost underneath
Vancouver's Granville Street Bridge, is Canada's oldest microbrewery.

Like the founding of Horseshoe Bay Brewery and Spinnakers, the
creation of the Granville Island Brewing Company involved a trans-
atlantic trip and the discovery of high-quality styles of beers not available
in Canada. In the later 1970s, Granville Island was being transformed
from a dingy industrial location to one featuring a covered market, restaurants, art shops, and studios, and Mitch Taylor, who had been one of
the builders of a marina there, had discovered unpasteurized lagers while
visiting small German towns. "I remember getting on the plane back
home and being annoyed that, after enjoying all those wonderful beers,
all I could get to drink was a mainstream Canadian lager."

Taylor and his partner, Bill Harvey, decided to build a brewery that
would produce German-style beers brewed according to the *Reinheitsgebot*,
the sixteenth-century Bavarian law that limited ingredients in beer to
water, hops, malted grain (usually barley), and later, when its presence was
discovered, yeast. This was a "law" that the megabrewers in Canada and
the US, who often substituted rice or corn for malt, hadn't been observing
for decades. The two men raised 2.5 million dollars in start-up money,

chose a location—a former paper warehouse clearly visible to visitors as they arrived at the now-fashionable Granville Island—and began the difficult tasks of dealing with provincial and federal regulations and of finding a brewmaster who could create the kinds of beers they wanted.

"We decided to sell on draft to pubs in the Vancouver area, which wasn't a problem. But we also wanted to sell bottles at the brewery. BC liquor laws had been changed to permit wineries to retail their products from their wineries. We wanted to do the same with beer but the problem was federal excise law, which would have meant that we'd have to brew and sell in different locations. We got that law changed. After we'd opened, we approached the provincial Liquor Control Board about selling in the government liquor stores. They said we'd have to place our bottled beers in every store in the province and we didn't have the capacity to produce that much beer, but they relented and we entered selected markets."

Finding a brewer trained in brewing unpasteurized German lagers was also difficult. "We couldn't find anyone in North America suitable for the job," Taylor said. So they turned to Germany, hiring Rainer Kullahne, a graduate of the Berlin School of Brewing. After his interview in Vancouver, Kullahne took a sample of Vancouver water back home with him, analyzed it, and found that it was ideal for the kinds of beers Granville Island wanted.

In late June 1984, Granville Island Brewing opened. The facility featured a taproom, a retail store, and a glass-walled brewery that was visible to customers. The first product was the now-famous Island Lager, a gold-coloured beer with malty notes and a crisp finish. It was followed by three others in the lager tradition—a winter bock, a light lager, and a marzen. Granville Island didn't enter the ale market until four years later; by then, West Coast-style pale ales from the US had become popular with Canadians visiting across the border.

Because Granville Island's beer was unfiltered, it had a much shorter shelf life than Molson, Labatt, and Carling-O'Keefe products. That was not generally a problem; by the end of the summer the brewery was struggling to keep up with increasing demand for its beer. "But, we made sure people knew that if their beer went bad, they could bring it back and exchange it for fresh beer," Taylor said. That didn't happen very often.

In 1985, Ed McNally, pictured here with daughter Shelagh, founded Big Rock Brewery, which is now the second-largest wholly Canadian-owned brewery.

Just as Spinnakers and Granville Island began offering their beers to delighted customers, Ed McNally, a Calgary corporate lawyer turned cattle breeder and barley farmer, began planning a brewery that would, he later said, produce the kinds of beers he liked to drink. These were not the pale, North American lagers churned out by the Alberta plants of Canada's national breweries. As the director of the Western Barley Growers Association, he knew that Alberta grew some of the best malting barley in the world and wondered why, if that were the case, Alberta breweries weren't making better beer.

As his daughter Shelagh McNally told it, Ed McNally's idea for starting a brewery came to him during a family vacation to Hawaii. "On the plane on the way over, he was reading a magazine article about the microbrewing movement in the United States. A couple of days later, when we were all at the beach, he ordered a mini-can of Budweiser to quench his thirst. He took one sip, spat it out, and emptied the rest of the can into the ocean. He thought that it tasted as bad as most of the stuff he could get back home." After spitting out the Budweiser, McNally realized that if he wanted good Alberta beer, he'd better start a brewery. He wasn't a homebrewer. In fact, his one attempt at it, when he was a university student, had ended in disaster. The brew blew up and when his landlady arrived home and saw what had happened to her basement suite, she suggested that McNally find new accommodations—quickly.

During the early 1980s, McNally and his friend Otto Leverkus rounded up investors, purchased and renovated an old warehouse, and hired Bernd Pieper, who had been classically trained in Europe and had worked with Guinness in Liberia and with Lowenbrau in Zurich. They chose not to go head-to-head against Molson, Labatt, or Carling-O'Keefe by producing a pale North American lager, or against such imported products as Guinness, Lowenbrau, Heineken, or Pilsner Urquell. They would use Alberta's hard water to create ales free of adjuncts, grains such as corn and rice, that were substituted for more expensive barley malt.

In September 1985, the new brewery, named Big Rock after an eighteen-thousand-ton glacial erratic rock on McNally's farm, released its first three ales, each of them in the British tradition: a dark ale named Traditional, an English bitter, and a porter. Of these, only the first is still brewed. Dark and full-flavoured without being aggressive or threatening, Traditional was something very different from what most Alberta drinkers were used to. Years later, Mike Tymchuk of Wild Rose Brewery acknowledged other microbrewers' debt to Big Rock in making Albertans aware of a new kind of beer. "Traditional did the heavy lifting in the early years," he said. "It taught Albertans not to be afraid of the dark."

During the 1980s, eighteen brewpubs and microbreweries opened in BC and Alberta. Most of them, including Troller Pub and Horseshoe Bay Brewery, plagued by financial difficulties, brewing problems, and/ or distribution obstacles, did not survive. In addition to Spinnakers, Granville Island (purchased by Molson in 2009), and Big Rock, three others—Vancouver Island Brewery in Victoria, Okanagan Spring in Vernon (now owned by Sleeman Brewery, a subsidiary of Sapporo of Japan), and Whistler—operated in 2010.

In the 1980s, Spinnakers, Big Rock, and Granville Island succeeded by introducing western Canadian beer drinkers to ales and lagers as they were meant to be. Meanwhile, the megabreweries were changing: during that decade they received the Canadian rights to brew Budweiser, Miller High Life, and Coors, introducing Canadian drinkers to infinitesimally different versions of a style they already knew very well: adjunct-added, pale North American lagers.

Alberta

Part One
Alberta

Between 1882, when the Saskatchewan Brewery opened in Medicine Hat in what was then the Northwest Territories, and 1916, when Prohibition was imposed on Albertans, sixteen breweries operated in the province: six in Calgary, four in Lethbridge, three in Edmonton, two in Medicine Hat, and one in Fort Macleod. Most were short-lived. However, four operated until late in the twentieth century.

Founded in 1892, Calgary Brewing and Malting operated independently until 1961, when it was purchased by Canadian Breweries Limited, a company operated by E.P. Taylor that had been acquiring breweries across Canada since the 1930s. It operated under Taylor's Carling brand until 1989, when Molson purchased Carling-O'Keefe. Five years later Molson closed the plant, concentrating their Alberta operations in Edmonton.

Two years after Calgary Brewing and Malting opened, Edmonton's Strathcona Brewing and Malting began to operate on the south side of the North Saskatchewan River. It later became the Northwest Brewing Company. Calgary Brewing and Malting purchased the brewery in 1952, renaming it Bohemian Maid. After Canadian Breweries purchased the Calgary company, the Edmonton plant became O'Keefe and then Carling-O'Keefe. It closed in 1975.

In 1903, Edmonton Brewing and Malting opened on the north side of the North Saskatchewan River. A decade later it moved a couple of miles away from the river, to the north side of town, and in 1927 was purchased by Fritz Sick, who, with his son Emil, went on to establish breweries in Saskatchewan, Alberta, British Columbia, and Washington State. In 1959, Sick sold the plant to Molson, which operated it until 2007.

The purchase of Edmonton Brewing and Malting was Sick's second Alberta venture. In 1901, he had founded Alberta Brewery (later named Lethbridge Brewing and Malting) in Lethbridge. The Sick family operated the plant until 1958, when they sold it to Molson, which closed it in 1989 after the merger with Carling-O'Keefe.

Older Alberta drinkers wax nostalgic about these breweries, speaking fondly of Bohemian Maid, Lethbridge Old Style, and Calgary Export Ale—beers that seem to become better the longer it has been since they were last brewed.

CHAPTER ONE

Lagers and Beyond
Edmonton to Red Deer

It is estimated that 90 per cent of the beer consumed in Alberta is lager, nearly all of it brewed by the multinationals Labatt and Molson Coors. However, of the more than five dozen types of beer brewed by Alberta's microbreweries and brewpubs, only eighteen are lagers, and most of these are not pale, North American-style lagers. Preferring to leave the megabrewers to do what they do best, and more cheaply than any microbrewer could, the microbreweries have produced such different types of lagers as a *helles* (Alley Kat's Charlie Flint's), a black pilsner (Jasper Brewing and Brew Brothers), and an Australian pepper berry-flavoured lager (Amber's). Three microbreweries have focused on lagers: Yellowhead of Edmonton, Roughneck of Calmar, and Drummond of Red Deer.

❖

Since it opened on Edmonton's south side in 1964, the **Labatt** brewery has dominated the Alberta brewing scene. Intended then as the crown jewel in the Ontario brewer's westward expansion, it has been enlarged frequently and now occupies two large city blocks, stretching from 99th Street on the east almost to Gateway Boulevard on the west. In 2007, when Molson closed its Edmonton facility, this became the largest brewery between Toronto and Vancouver. It produces Labatt Blue, a pale lager that was one of Canada's first national beers, along with the discount brand Lucky Lager and, since 1980, Budweiser and later Bud Light, the most widely consumed lagers in the world.

The company still bears the name it acquired shortly after John Labatt bought a London, Ontario, brewery in the middle of the nineteenth century. However, in 1995, Interbrew, a Belgian firm, purchased Labatt. Nine years later, Interbrew merged with AmBev of Brazil to become InBev, and in 2008, InBev merged with Anheuser-Busch to become Anheuser-Busch-InBev, a global brewing giant employing over three hundred thousand people worldwide and producing more than three hundred brands of beer.

For many years, a giant can of Labatt Blue sat atop one of the roofs of the brewery's Edmonton facility. In 2009, it was replaced by a can of Bud Light, now the biggest-selling beer in Alberta.

The south Edmonton plant still produces Blue, but Budweiser and Bud Light now account for 85 per cent of its 1.6 million hectolitres annual production. The iconic American "King of Beers" is brewed to rigid specifications, and the St. Louis head office conducts weekly tests on samples of the beers expressed from around the world. The Bud consumed in Alberta and British Columbia must taste the same as one quaffed in the United States, Europe, Asia, South America, and Africa.

In 2007, Bud Light replaced Kokanee, a Labatt product from BC, as the most popular beer in Alberta. Its growing status and the decline in the fortunes of Labatt Blue are symbolized by the replacement in 2009 of the twenty-five-foot-high Labatt Blue can, which had stood atop one of the brewery buildings for many years, by a Bud Light can.

To many beer drinkers, there is little difference in flavour among Budweiser, Molson Canadian, and Labatt Blue, the major North American lagers produced by the two megabrewers. To discover Edmonton brewers producing different lagers, ones with more flavour, it is necessary to proceed north along 99th Street to the locations of two of Edmonton's three microbreweries: Alley Kat and Amber's.

Neil Herbst, founder of Edmonton's Alley Kat Brewing Company, displays several of the awards the company has garnered.

❖

Only a small sign at the southwest corner of 99th Street and 60th Avenue indicates the nearby presence of **Alley Kat Brewing Company,** Edmonton's oldest, and Alberta's second oldest (Calgary's Big Rock has been around since 1985), microbrewery. In 1994, award-winning home-brewer Neil Herbst took a buyout from his job with the downsizing Alberta government and joined Richard Cholon to start a microbrewery. "We were very optimistic," he later said about his decision to turn his hobby into a profession. "I thought everyone shared the passion I had for good beer. And we underestimated the costs of starting up and over-estimated our skills."

They chose the name Alley Kat because "both Richard and I had cats and Alley Kat sounded a little like a British pub name. It was also a bit out there." The cat theme was carried into the names of many of their beers: Aprikat, Razzykat, and Olde Deuteronomy (from a character in the Broadway musical *Cats*). The early labels had cartoon drawings of cats, and their advertising tag line was "Great Beers— From Scratch."

ALLEY KAT

APRIKAT

raft Brewed Beer

A delicate and unique wheat a
the fresh taste of orchard p

Beer/Bière • 341ml.
onton, Alberta by A

Their first two beers, an amber lager and an unfiltered wheat beer, appeared in January 1995 and were an attempt to help Alberta beer drinkers cross over from the mainstream lagers of the megabrewers. "I think we were a bit naive about what the public was ready for," Herbst said in retrospect. The wheat beer may have been similar in colour to the beers the majority of Albertans were drinking, but, because it was unfiltered, it had a cloudiness that people weren't used to. And the amber was much too dark for a lager.

Although both beers disappeared within a few years, Scona Gold, the lager, went out in triumph, winning both a silver medal at the 1997 World Beer Championships and notoriety. The same year, it was specially packaged for an Edmonton liquor store as Brew-X, with a label showing a parachute-less man jumping from a plane flying over a jungle. The implicit reference was to the Bre-X scandal, in which an Alberta businessman had reportedly "fallen" from a helicopter after he had accepted twenty million dollars worth of investments for a worthless Indonesian mine. A Calgary newspaper expressed indignation, calling the label tasteless.

After a year or two, Herbst began to develop the four beer styles that are still the core of the brewery's offerings: Charlie Flint's Lager (an organic beer named after a pioneering Alberta brewer), Full Moon Pale Ale, Amber Ale, and Aprikat (a fruit-flavoured beer cooler). He began by studying the style guidelines for each beer he wanted to make and then "started from scratch," creating his recipes and brewing several small test batches until he'd found just what he was aiming for.

About Charlie Flint's, which, along with Aprikat, is Alley Kat's best seller, he remarked, "We wanted a lager that would be different from the mainstream ones so popular in Alberta, but not so over-the-top that it would scare new drinkers away." He compared it to a European *helles* lager, more golden than straw yellow, with fuller malt flavours, and more—but not overwhelming—hoppiness than mainstream lagers.

Aprikat, light amber in colour and light-bodied, has a refreshing effervescence and an apricot taste that becomes more evident with more sips. Contrary to some people's opinion, it isn't just for women drinkers. Herbst recounted how Cholon was once approached in a bar by a motorcyclist wearing chains, adorned with tattoos, and carrying a bottle of Aprikat. To Cholon's surprise, the beer drinker praised the product, commenting knowledgeably about its various traits.

Amber Ale and Full Moon Pale Ale are what Herbst calls "the yin and yang of our beers." The former emphasizes malt flavours, the latter hops. The crystal and chocolate malts used in the Amber give a complexity of flavours to the red- to amber-coloured, full-bodied smooth ale. The Pale Ale, styled after a beer made famous by Sierra Nevada Brewery of Chico, California, is noticeably but not overwhelming hoppy.

In addition to the regular offerings, the brewery produces a number of seasonal and special-release beers. "One of the advantages of being small," Herbst explained, "is that we can experiment with lesser-known styles, experimenting and producing small batches. If something doesn't work, we haven't invested too much time and money."

Many of the special brews have had such interesting additives as cinnamon, nutmeg, and cardamom, as well as fruit extracts like raspberry, orange, pumpkin, and cherry. Some of the most unusual specials have been a garlic beer and a chili beer. Herbst placed a small garlic clove and a jalapeño pepper inside each bottle of those respective beers.

Although each Alley Kat product is designed to be a unique example of its particular style, taken together, the beers give the brewery a distinct house character. "You could say that we're a bit quirky. We have a lot of fun, but we take what we do seriously. We pay a great deal of attention to quality and consistency, testing our recipes until they're where we want them to be in terms of having a high flavour profile. Edmonton's water, which is neither too hard nor too soft, gives a mineral taste to our beers."

❖❖❖

Eighteen blocks north of Alley Kat, again just off 99th Street, stands **Amber's Brewing Company**, the presence of which is indicated only by a small sign that is nearly hidden by a boulevard tree.

"A friend and I had wanted to start an alcoholic-cooler facility," said Jim Gibbon, the brewery's owner. "But we found out that in Alberta, you could only brew coolers as a sideline to a brewery business. So I formed Amber's Brewing. I wanted to create a company that would be for Edmonton what Big Rock Brewery was for Calgary. We set out to be Edmontonians making beer for Edmontonians." Amber, whose name

is given to the brewery, is a fictional character based on women from Edmonton's past: Gibbon's grandmother, who motorcycled around the province with her husband in the 1920s, and the Edmonton Five, a group of local women who fought for women's suffrage.

Gibbon began business in 2006 with two brews: Australian Mountain Pepper Berry Lager and a honey brown ale (since dropped). Initially, he had his recipes contract-brewed by Alley Kat, but he soon realized that he would need to have his own brewery if the business were to grow. That's when he met Joe Parrell, a Newfoundlander who, many years earlier, had helped his father homebrew and later taken a course from London's Institute of Brewing and Distilling, before working at Molson's Edmonton brewery. "I learned all I know about beer there. I worked in quality control and studied how to test a brew at every stage of the process. I learned the importance of keeping all the equipment, all the brewery, spotless. You spend 80 per cent of your time cleaning."

However, working for a megabrewery that held countless meetings deprived Parrell of much creative work. He'd met Gibbon in the summer of 2007, just before Molson announced that it was closing the Edmonton plant and moving all western production to Vancouver. He tendered his resignation and joined Gibbon, putting together a new brewing system, tinkering with old recipes, and developing new ones. He stayed with the brewery until 2010.

Amber's now creates four different beers: two lagers, a pale ale, and a stout. Gibbon decided on Australian Mountain Pepper Berry Lager after he tasted the slightly fruity and peppery dried fruits his sister-in-law brought back from an Australian vacation. The flavours they would impart to a beer would give just the right difference to the lager he intended to brew. Parrell brewed a pilsner-style lager that provided a contrast to the flavour of the additives. "It's not too sweet and it's lightly hopped, so that it finishes clean and crisp."

Sap Vampire Maple Lager is boldly distinctive. "I spent weeks think-ing about a name," Gibbon said. "It's got maple syrup in it and sap is like the blood of a tree. So why not vampire?" The packaging is designed to draw the attention of a customer surveying shelves of beer: against a dark red background is the silhouette of a bat flying toward a tree. There's more than just a hint of maple syrup in every sip. "Someone told

Joe Parrell (left), former brewer for Amber's, and owner Jim Gibbon display
two of the unusually decorated cartons in which the beers are packaged.

me it made them think of a pancake breakfast on Sunday morning,"
remarked Gibbon. "I jokingly said that maybe you could design your
meals around our beers, starting with Sap Vampire in the morning and
ending with our Kenmount Road Chocolate Stout for a nightcap." Joe
Parrell said that he used a type of malt that produced a sweeter flavour
and took advantage of Amber's fire-brewing process to create a fuller-
bodied, richer beer.

Bub's Lunch Pail Ale is dry-hopped—that is, more hops are added
during the fermenting stages—and a small amount of wheat is added to
increase the head. The finished product has more noticeable hop aromas
and flavours. The "Bub" of the name refers to the big-nosed hero of an
Edmonton comic strip from the 1980s. "Bub is a blue-collar worker. He
wears a hard hat and he's a proud Edmontonian," Gibbon noted. He and
Parrell referred to the product as "the beer with the big nose," a reference
not only to the prominent hop aromas but to the comic strip character's
most noticeable facial feature.

Kenmount Road Chocolate Stout is named after an important
thoroughfare in Parrell's home town of St. John's, Newfoundland.

"I'm very proud of this beer. It's my own recipe and it celebrates my hometown. I wanted a stout with a chocolate flavour, something not too heavy, but not thin." The very dark beverage balances chocolate, coffee, nut, and caramel flavours. "It's as hearty as a Jigs dinner [a traditional Newfoundland meal that includes corned beef, cabbage, and other vegetables], but you can also enjoy it with Alberta beef and, technically, happy hour starts half an hour earlier," Parrell suggested.

Describing what he sees as Amber's profile in Alberta's brewing landscape, Gibbon began by stating, "We aren't in competition with either the megabreweries or Alley Kat. Molson and Labatt do what they do very well and, because of their size, they can offer their products at a lower price than we can. And Alley Kat creates some of the best beers in the country. We're trying to complement them. We offer distinct options: wild and spicy, sweet and smooth, hoppy and chocolatey beers. Our names are creative and so are our beers."

❖

Yellowhead Brewing Company, which opened in May 2010, is located in an historic downtown Edmonton building that briefly housed Maverick Brewing during the first decade of the twenty-first century. Owner Gene Dub, an Edmonton architect, was delighted to find a good business to occupy the 1913 building and expressed his belief that, even though the previous tenants had failed, there was certainly room for a downtown brewery in the city. "Maverick tried to get too big too fast," he said. "We want to be small, to start by serving the downtown community."

Dub felt that it was important to begin with one style of beer, establish it firmly in the minds of local beer drinkers and then, perhaps, add other styles. "We decided to start selling on draft, to keep expenses down, although we will have half-litre bottles available for sale at the brewery and in liquor stores."

To create the beers, Dub hired a person highly trained in the German lager tradition, Scott Harris, who had studied at the respected Doemens Technicum of Munich and then worked in the brewery of the Bavarian royal family. An Edmonton native, Harris hadn't intended to become a brewer; in fact, he'd enjoyed a distinguished career as a soloist with ballet

Scott Harris, brewmaster for Yellowhead Brewing,
pours the brewery's first "official" pitcher of lager.

companies, first in Alberta and then in Munich, before a back injury forced him into early retirement. "Because it was a work-related injury, the German government offered to retrain me. I was sitting having a beer, wondering what I'd do when I looked at the bottle and realized that brewing would be a very interesting career."

When he began his training, Harris's dream was to return to Alberta to open a brewery, and that partially came true when he founded Banff Brewing. However, regulations prevented him from brewing the maple amber ale he created—"Something I knew that tourists would find very Canadian"—in the park. When difficulties arose with having it contract-brewed to his specifications, he put Banff Brewing on hiatus. He saw an advertisement for a brewer in his hometown, applied for the job, was accepted, and began to design a recipe for the first beer.

"Most microbrewers start with ales, which are quicker and easier to make than lagers, and they don't want to go head-on against the lagers of the 'biggies.' But I thought, 'Most people in Alberta drink lagers, and there isn't a lot of good lager around.'" He turned to his German training and developed what he wanted to be an Edmonton interpretation of a Munich *helles*—a clear, golden, naturally carbonated lager that was more malty and slightly less hoppy than Czech lagers. "People here are still not into hops; they don't like their beer to be bitter." Harris noted that he may up the quantity of the malt in the recipe to give the beer more body. "We don't want it to be thin like the biggies' beer."

Yellowhead was officially opened on May 19, 2010, with Dean Neil Gordon of Edmonton's All Saints Cathedral blessing the brewery, performing a six-hundred-year-old ceremony designed to bring success. He explained that in the early days of brewing, when the scientific reasons for success or failure of a batch of beer were not understood, a bad brew was often attributed to evil spiritual forces. A priest's blessing would keep those negative powers away and ensure the well-being of the brewery and, by extension, the community in which it was operating.

Brewsters Brewing Company and Restaurant—Oliver Square is four blocks east of Yellowhead's city-centre facility. It contains the brewing equipment for the five Edmonton locations of the Calgary-headquartered chain. Like the other restaurants in the chain, it has a standard menu and beer list, and the facility is divided into a family restaurant and adults-only pub. (A full description of Brewsters, their beers and their menus is found on pages 45 to 49.)

Roughneck Brewing Company is housed in a small building in a corner of the Cameron Brothers Trucking Company yard, which is just outside

Terry Cameron is the owner, brewmaster, and frequently
sole employee of Roughneck Brewing Company.

the small town of Calmar, thirty kilometres southwest of the sprawling
Labatt complex in Edmonton. Terry Cameron, the owner, brewmaster, and, at times, the only employee of Roughneck, is a homebrewer
who, when he became tired of the gruelling life of an oil patch worker,
contemplated starting his own beer company. He purchased brewing
equipment that had been used in Rayne, Louisiana, stored it, began the
long process of applying for and then waiting for a brewing licence and
zoning approval from the county, and started to build a structure to
house the new project.

In December 2004, his progress was halted. Official approvals had arrived, but a sudden storm from the north flattened the partially completed building. "We picked the pieces up and started to rebuild." He created and worked on his recipes, brewed several test batches, and made his first sale, a golden ale, in October 2007. "I started with an ale, because ales are quicker and easier to make." He began selling a lager in June 2008 and a brown ale in the winter of 2009. He did not see himself in competition with the large breweries, but as the provider of an alternative for the beer drinkers he sought to serve.

Cameron's target audience was the rural, relatively young, lager-drinking population of central Alberta. The name of the company, as well as the names of the ale, Driller's, and the lager, Pipeline, were designed to appeal to this market, as was the advertising tag line, "Play Rough, Drink Smooth." He also decided to make his brews available on draft and in cans. "The initial outlay for cans was pretty big, but it turned out to be cheaper than bottles in the long run. And rural people are used to their beer in cans, not bottles."

To make inroads into the market, he had to develop beverages that didn't duplicate those of the megabrewers, but that weren't so different as to frighten drinkers away. "I remember when I was working on the ale. I kept thinking, 'Take it easy on the hops; don't make it too dark; make it medium-bodied. Don't make it threatening.'" Driller's Ale has achieved his goals. It's medium golden, with a mild hop taste and a medium body, the kind of beer that traditional beer drinkers would find an easy transition from the pale North American lagers they are used to. In fact, Cameron said, "People told me that they had expected something really different, but it wasn't—and they meant that as a compliment. People appreciated that we were local and that we bought local malt."

Getting acceptance of Pipeline Lager was more difficult. If he were to acquire a share of the rural central Alberta market, he would have to do it with a lager. "I had to work at the flavour, finding something that people would accept," Cameron noted. "I tweaked the recipe, using different yeasts and trying different fermentation processes. Initially, the beer was too dark. It was a Vienna style, and people thought it had too much body. But I seem to have found what people wanted and after a year, it started to sell well. There aren't any adjuncts and we don't pasteurize it. People are saying to

When they started their brewery in Red Deer, partners Kevin Wood (left) and Cody Geddes-Bachman decided to name it Drummond, after one of the city's earlier breweries.

me, 'That's how a lager should taste.'" It's not as pale as a mainstream lager, has a slightly fuller body, and a stronger, but still understated, hop taste.

In the winter of 2009, Cameron began testing a third brew, a brown ale, something very different from what his customers were used to. But, like his other two beers, it wasn't full-bodied or too hoppy, and it wasn't aggressive with its malt flavours. "People have responded well at tastings I've put on, and it's now available on draft." In the fall of 2010, he released the brown ale and an English-style India Pale Ale, under the label Brewmaster's Choice.

❖❖❖

Unlike Terry Cameron of Roughneck, Cody Geddes-Bachman and Kevin Wood, owners of Red Deer's **Drummond Brewing Company**, decided to go head-to-head with the multinationals rather than seek their place in the niche markets of the microbrewers.

The two had been importing beer that they'd had brewed for them in Wisconsin and sold in Alberta as Silver Springs. But in 2006, when the Alberta government reduced the tax for small breweries from thirty-one cents to three cents a litre, they decided to move production back to Canada. Red Deer seemed to be an ideal location for their brewery: the area population was around 200,000 and the nearest breweries were an hour-and-a-half drive away. When they discovered that Sleeman Brewery, which had bought the equipment and trademarks of the Drummond Brewery after it had gone under in 1995, had allowed the trademarks to lapse, they decided to resurrect the name.

"My father drank Drummond. It was a good beer and a respected brand in central Alberta. People were sorry when production stopped. We felt that would be a good first step in being noticed," Wood explained. They then tracked down Wolfgang Hoess, the Vienna-trained brewer who'd been in charge of production during Drummond's first incarnation. "He knew what the local people liked, and he knew how to get the most out of the local water, which was ideal for lagers."

The two owners decided that to succeed in what Wood called a market of "old-school drinkers"—that is, consumers of North American pale lagers—they would be wise to start with a lager "that wasn't too radical a departure from local tastes." They experimented, lowering the amount of German hops in their recipes, making Drummond Lager more like what the old-school drinkers expected. But there was one way in which the lager they offered was significantly different from that of their very big competitors: it had no adjuncts—just malt, hops, water, and yeast. Moreover, it was unpasteurized and contained no preservatives. It was delivered fresh, on draft and in cans, to bars and liquor stores. "Fresh beer," Wood emphasized, "is everything."

In addition, it was local. Geddes-Bachman worked to establish the brewery's presence in the city, sponsoring sports teams and offering tastings at area bars and liquor stores. Within eight months of Drummond's opening in September 2008, it was running at full capacity and had plans to add more equipment. Although it is available from Edmonton to Calgary, the prime market remains Red Deer and the small hotels in the rural areas nearby. "We want to establish ourselves firmly in our own backyard. But our goal is to become the third largest brewery in Alberta, behind Labatt and Big Rock."

Labatt Breweries of Canada
   10119 45th Ave, Edmonton, T6E 3Z7, 780-436-6060, labatt.com
Alley Kat Brewing Company
   9929 60th Ave, Edmonton, T6E 0C7, 780-436-8922, alleykatbeer.com
Amber's Brewing Company
   9926 78th Ave, Edmonton, T6E 1N5, 780-628-2305, ambersbrewing.com
Yellowhead Brewing Company
   10229 105th St, Edmonton, T5J 1E3, 780-423-3333
Brewsters Brewing Company and Restaurant, brewsters.ca
   Castledowns
      15327 Castledowns Rd, Edmonton, T5X 6C3, 780-425-4677
   Century Park
      2335 111th St, Edmonton, T6J 5E5, 780-429-4677
   Meadow Lark
      15820 87th Ave, Edmonton, T5R 5W9, 780-421-4677
   Oliver Square
      11620 104th Ave, Edmonton, T5K 2T7, 780-482-4677
   Summerside
      1140 91st St, Edmonton, T6X 0P2, 780-424-4677
Roughneck Brewing Company
   PO Box 732, Calmar, T0C 0V0, 780-499-0691, roughneckbrewing.com
Drummond Brewing Company
   8 - 6610 71st St, Red Deer, T4P 3Y7, 403-346-1146, drummondbeer.com

Rocky Mountain Brews and Views
Calgary to Jasper

Thirty kilometres north of Calgary, in a farmer's field next to Highway 2, stand three-metre-high cans of three varieties of Big Rock beer. They tend to list a little, like three buddies heading home after an evening at the local tavern. The cans are less than half the size of the one that is on the roof of the Labatt brewery in Edmonton, but they're very noticeable. And they're not actually cans, but plastic wrapped around upright bales of hay.

They're the brainchild of Shelagh McNally, daughter of Ed, the founder of **Big Rock Brewery**, the province's largest and oldest independent brewery. "We couldn't afford the kind of television advertising that Labatt and Molson have, and this seemed a different way to bring our product to the attention of Albertans. They only cost six hundred dollars each and a few cases of beer for the farmer. We have them beside the main highways leading into Calgary and Edmonton. They're very popular. Farmers are asking us to put them on their land. One has been stolen, and a cow knocked another over to get at the hay inside."

From a modest beginning in 1985 of three kegs a week, Big Rock's production expanded rapidly. By 1988, it was brewing fifteen thousand hectolitres annually and had begun exporting to other provinces and several American states. Although it was winning converts because of the distinctive flavours and the quality of the beer, several fortuitous events also contributed to its growth. In June 1986, just as the brewery began to market its new pale ale, Labatt, Molson, and Carling-O'Keefe went on strike in Alberta and the weather turned hot. Then in 1988, officials and media attending the Calgary Winter Olympics discovered Big Rock beers, were favourably impressed, and spread the word around the city and, later, back home. Shortly afterwards, the late Michael Jackson, an internationally acclaimed beer connoisseur, displayed a bottle of McNally's Extra Irish Ale, a 7 per cent ABV Irish ale, on the cover of his *New World Guide to Beer* and called it one of the fourteen best beers he'd tasted.

Without the enormous budgets of the megabreweries, officials of
Calgary's Big Rock Brewery decided to draw attention to their products
by placing large beer cans in fields next to major highways.

During the 1990s, production increased so much that the owners decided to build a new brewery, one with the capacity to brew close to half a million hectolitres a year. In 1996, the new plant opened, complete with a state-of-the-art canning line—a machine that enabled Big Rock to ship more beer more cheaply, and to have it arrive fresher at its destination. Located on what was then the eastern edge of Calgary, the new brewery was laid out, Shelagh McNally commented, to resemble an Alberta farmyard. "There's a windbreak of trees around the edge of the property. The administration building [which also houses an independent restaurant, Big Rock Grill, and function rooms that are rented out] is like the farmhouse. The brewery, across a courtyard from the farmhouse, is like the animal barn, and the bottling and storage building is like the machine barn."

Now an established veteran, no longer a microbrewery but a regional, producing over two hundred and twenty thousand hectolitres a year, its beers available in all Canadian provinces but Quebec and

Prince Edward Island, Big Rock is the second-largest wholly Canadian brewery, next only to Moosehead of New Brunswick. The brewery has a core list of nine beers and each year it produces a few seasonal and special edition brews.

Paul Gautreau, vice-president of operations, head brewer, and former Carling-O'Keefe employee, "knocked on Big Rock's door in 1986, seeking work because they were brewing the kind of ales I was trying to make at home." He spoke enthusiastically about the company's lineup, commenting first on how Traditional's nutty flavour and "nice sweetness" balance the hops, making the drink neither too dry nor too bitter. After a quarter of a century, Traditional remains Big Rock's best-selling product. Grasshopper, a wheat ale, originally intended to be a summer seasonal when it was introduced in the early 1990s, took off quickly and has consistently sold well, in both summer and winter. "Trad is a bigger seller in the winter, but Grasshopper takes over in the summer," Gautreau remarked. Named after the insect that, Big Rock's website reports tongue-in-cheek, smashed into Ed McNally's windshield the day he had the inspiration to produce a wheat beer, it is "a great patio beer, lighter in flavour than our other beers." It is fully filtered and pours a crystal-clear, golden yellow, unlike many other wheat beers, which have a yeast haze to them. "When we're processing in the mash tun, it makes me think of bread-making." Saaz hops give a light, not bitter, flavour to the drink.

XO Lager, the first Big Rock beer to compete directly with the megabrewers' lagers, is different from theirs because it uses no adjuncts. "It's all malts and is complemented with Saaz hops from the Czech Republic. It doesn't need to be sweet and the important thing is in the hopping; it must be correct. It was a challenge for us to create." It was originally produced in the early 1990s and marked Big Rock's first big move away from being a competitor to the imports to becoming a player in the larger Alberta beer market.

In 2010, Big Rock added Gopher Lager to its lineup. Announced as a North American all-malt lager, it uses pale malts and only Saaz hops to provide a non-threatening taste. It appears to have been designed as a crossover beer, something that has a flavour more familiar to drinkers of mainstream lagers than does XO.

Gautreau called McNally's Extra Irish Ale, "the best beer we make. It's strong and full-flavoured, a notch above Trad. The malts contribute a fruitiness and currant flavours. It has a fantastic mouth-feel. It's a balance of alcohol content—7 per cent ABV—and flavour. The hops are tasted throughout the experience of taking a sip. When we were recognized by Michael Jackson, it was our proudest moment."

Big Rock's other brews are, in a sense, niche beers. Warthog, a mild, brown cream ale, is lighter in alcohol (4.5 per cent) and not so full-bodied, but with a little more pronounced hop bitterness. "I sometimes refer to it as 'Trad Light,'" Gautreau remarked. Black Amber Ale is like a sweet stout, while Jack Rabbit Light, a 3.8 per cent ABV lager, is an all-malt beverage that offers an alternative to drinkers of mainstream light lagers.

Big Rock Lime, introduced as a summer 2009 seasonal, exemplifies the meaning of one of the company's earlier advertising lines: "Beer that tastes like beer." In 2007, Miller had produced Chill, a citrus beer for the American market, and a year later Anheuser-Busch came out with Bud Lime. Rumours circulated that Bud Lime was scheduled for Canadian release in 2010, and Paul Gautreau and his fellow brewers began to develop their own version of the beer for 2009. "Big Rock Lime is different from the American types of the style, which we felt were too limey and sweet. We wanted only a slight aroma and taste of lime. We created a different recipe than that for Jack Rabbit—4 per cent as opposed to 3.8 per cent ABV and a little maltier than Jack Rabbit. We also used different hops."

Anheuser-Busch, which may have found out about Big Rock's plans, decided to launch its lime beer in the late spring of 2009 and began shipping product from its brewery in England. It was popular and supplies were quickly exhausted. Fortuitously, Big Rock launched its Lime two days before the official beginning of summer and just as the Budweiser stock had run dry. Within a week, demand for Big Rock Lime pushed production facilities to the limit. Big Rock dominated the prairie market for the summer-style beer and it was made a year-round offering.

Six kilometres to the west, on 11th Avenue, downtown Calgary's famous "Electric Avenue," **Brew Brothers Brewery** has six metres of public

Alan Yule checks on the latest batch of beer he's brewing for Calgary's Brew Brothers.

exposure. "People walking by can see our mash tun, brew kettle, and lauter tun when they look through the window of the building we're in, but most of the work is done in the cellar," explains current brewer Alan Yule, a former geologist who was a founding partner of Calgary's third microbrewery, Wild Rose.

Brew Brothers opened in 1994 when the five members of the Marquis de Suds, a local homebrewing club, decided, in the words of Brad LeDrew, that "we were brewing such good beer we should try to sell it." The group made two important decisions. Initially, it would have the beers contract-brewed in order to avoid the high costs of setting up a brewery, and it would focus on lagers, not ales. "Big Rock had a strong line of ales. We decided not to compete, but to offer an alternative," LeDrew noted.

On a trip to the Czech Republic, he had visited the Pilsner Urquell brewery and tried their *dunkel*, a dark pilsner. Impressed, he decided that Black Pilsner would be Brew Brothers' first offering. Alberta beer drinkers were surprised and a little bewildered. "It didn't look like a lager; it looked like Guinness, but didn't taste like it," many of them said. Fifteen years later, it is Brew Brothers' most popular beer.

In 2005, Brew Brothers made the decision to do their own brewing. "We wanted to have a restaurant above the brewery, so we could serve directly from the cellar. But we didn't have the restaurant experience." The company sold the restaurant, which now does serve the beer directly from the cellar, and concentrated on building their draft market in Calgary and Edmonton.

Yule, who worked with Sleeman and Big Rock after leaving Wild Rose, said that Brew Brothers' beer was characterized by its balance between hops and malts, "the best friends in a beer." The beers do not have pronounced flavours, but subtle, modest relationships among the various malts, hops, and yeasts. In Black Pilsner, dark roasted malts and black malts, along with German hops and Czech pilsner yeast create a beer with a light body and a clear finish, one with more flavour than mainstream lagers. Tumbleweed Wheat, like Black Pilsner, has an alcohol level of 4.5 per cent ABV. "You don't need a lot of alcohol to give a beer flavour," Yule explained. The unfiltered wheat beer has a lemon-grapefruit finish. Ambush Pale Ale, at 5.5 per cent ABV, is the brewery's strongest beer but unlike India Pale Ale or West Coast-style pale ale, hops do not dominate. The East Golding hops, which impart an earthy, herbal taste, complement the crystal malts.

❖

If **Big Rock's** new premises were designed and grouped to resemble a traditional farm cluster, the building now housing Calgary's **Wild Rose Brewery** still looks the way it did when it was a Canadian Forces Quonset

Mike Tymchuk, founder of Wild Rose Brewery, dispenses
beer from one of the company's popular party pigs.

hut. Building 23 of Currie Barracks, once a military-clothing supply
depot, is close to what is now a trendy weekend farmers' market a half-
dozen kilometres southwest of Brew Brothers.

Founded by Mike Tymchuk and Alan Yule, Wild Rose began operations in 1996 in a Calgary industrial park. Tymchuk, who had worked
as a chef at Victoria's Spinnakers Gastro Brewpub in the 1980s, had
never been a homebrewer, but began his brewing education when the
Victoria establishment gave him the chance to create an eight hundred-
litre batch of beer. Over the next decade, he worked in Penticton,
Saskatoon, and Calgary, and consulted for breweries in China, Japan,
and the Philippines.

Wild Rose made its first sale, a keg of Brown Ale, in the fall of 1996.
It later moved to one-litre, stopper-style bottles and then, in 2006, to
341-millilitre bottles, sold in six-packs. The introduction of bottles
coincided with the move to Currie Barracks and marked a turning point
in the company's fortunes. "We started getting customers who'd been

doing Saturday shopping at the farmers' market. They'd visit our tap-room and restaurant [which serves such traditional pub food as meat pie and Roughneck's—i.e., ploughman's—Lunch] and later, when they saw our beers in liquor stores, they'd pick up a six-pack."

Tymchuk said that the brewery's success resulted not just from the move to Currie Barracks or the bottling of six-packs, but also from making beer that Albertans wanted to buy. "It isn't all that difficult to make good beer, but you have to know your market. In Victoria, people liked the English styles. When I developed Brewsters beers for the Brewsters brewpubs in Alberta, we were marketing to a crossover group and we didn't want to be too different. Then, when I worked with Mission Bridge Brewpub in Calgary, we were able to be a little more adventurous."

Wild Rose advances that sense of adventurousness. "We are a craft brewery that makes some of the 'wildest' beers in Canada," the compa-ny's website proclaims, "beers that are distinctive yet still approachable." This philosophy probably explains why Wild Rose does not brew any lagers. "Others do it well and much cheaper than we could," Tymchuk explained. "We open markets; we don't dive into existing ones. We don't sell to Molson and Labatt customers. We're not driven in every move by guidelines set down in style books. We see ourselves as style leaders."

Wild Rose has a core list of six beers, complemented by seasonals and special issues, and Friday-afternoon special release casks (available only at the Currie Barracks taproom). The initial four core beers were, as mar-keting manager Tina Wolfe described them, "The Dark," "The Fruit," "The Hoppy," and "The Foggie"—references to Brown Ale, Wrasberry Ale, India Pale Ale, and Velvet Fog, respectively. Since then, Wred Wheat Ale and S.O.B. Classic English Ale have been added to the list.

"The Dark," Tymchuk commented, "has been our workhorse. It carried the load for us during the difficult years, and it sells well all year." An ale with hints of chocolate and coffee, the hop bitterness balances, without overcoming, the malty sweetness. Medium-bodied, it has a crisp finish.

"The Fruit" is the Wrasberry Ale, Wild Rose's year-round bestseller, a raspberry-flavoured drink that, Tymchuk emphasized, is a beer, not a beer cooler. "We put whole raspberries into the fermentation tank, something not many others do. You can smell the berries, but get just a hint of their taste when you drink. We don't want the fruit flavour to overwhelm the beer."

"The Hoppy," India Pale Ale, originally called Industrial Park Ale in a reference to the brewery's first home, reflects the influence of Tymchuk's West Coast training. "It was a tough thing to do in Alberta, especially with the fairly high level of bitterness. Some people here think bitter is a four-letter word, and we had to introduce them to it gradually. We countered the bitterness by making our IPA maltier than most." It is also a hefty 6.0 per cent ABV.

"The Foggie," or Velvet Fog, the nickname given to Mel Tormé, the popular singer of the 1940s, refers to the visual quality of the beer. The first unfiltered wheat beer made from 100 per cent Alberta-grown wheat, it has a fuller, richer taste than filtered varieties. At first, beer drinkers protested: "If it ain't clear, it ain't beer." But they were soon won over and "The Foggie" became Wild Rose's top seller. The website offers instructions on how to enjoy the "velvetness" to the fullest, telling drinkers to swirl the bottle before pouring, putting the unfiltered yeast into suspension and enhancing both the visual and tasting experience. Wild Rose also brews a second wheat ale, Wréd Wheat Ale, which is stronger than Velvet Fog—5.0 per cent ABV as compared to Velvet Fog's 4.5 per cent—and darker, with a fuller body and a more malty flavour.

The sixth year-round offering is S.O.B., which is identified on the label as a Classic English Ale. The three initials refer to Special Old Bitter, a popular English session beer that can be enjoyed during an evening at the local pub. Given prevailing attitudes about bitterness in Alberta, Wild Rose decided to leave the six-letter "four-letter word," bitter, off the label. "It had to be hoppy, but not too much. We couldn't be more aggressive and succeed." It provides an example of Tymchuk's working to make his brewery a style leader in Alberta, trying something that is unfamiliar, but tweaking recipes so as not to alienate potential customers.

Of the fourteen brewpubs operating in Alberta, eleven are part of the **Brewsters Brewing Company and Restaurant** chain. Founded in Regina in the late 1980s by brothers Laurie, Marty, and Michael Lanigan, the company moved into Alberta in 1991, opening what was then the province's only brewpub on Calgary's 11th Avenue, just south of Calgary's downtown area. Over the next two decades, the company expanded greatly; in the summer of 2010 it operated three establishments in Regina, five in Calgary, five in Edmonton, and one in Airdrie, a rapidly growing town north of Calgary. "We locate in emerging areas and try to become part of the community," Lanigan remarked, noting that the company had considered moving to Airdrie for many years before opening in 2009. "We realized that there was a gap in an expanding community."

Each restaurant is divided into a family dining area, where children are welcome, and the pub, open only to adults. Because Alberta law permits beers brewed at one location to be shipped and sold at another brewpub owned by the same company, only two of the locations have breweries: Calgary's Foothills and Edmonton's Oliver Square.

The brewpub chain's website states that "the prime objective of Brewsters Brewing Company is to provide a genuine alternative for beer lovers who want to sample different styles of beer from around the world while enjoying our extensive menu designed to complement our handcrafted beers." Patrons can purchase the usual mainstream domestic beers and well-known imports, but most of the beer, available on tap and in 650-millilitre takeout bottles, is Brewsters' own. "Our beers aren't mainstream," Edmonton's Century Park manager Trevor Drane said, "but they aren't radically different in taste and aroma. With the exception of our bestsellers—River City Raspberry Ale and Blackfoot Blueberry Ale—you could call them crossover beers. They are similar to what people are used to, but with a difference." Edmonton brewmaster Gunther Trageser noted that "our variety should cater to everyone."

Both Drane and Calgary brewmaster Rob Walsh admitted that in a province where mainstream lagers are king, one of their jobs is to educate people about their different brands. "We have a wide variety of products, and we encourage people to enjoy a sampler tray—five five-ounce glasses—to find out which they like." The menu includes three lagers, three wheat ales, two fruit ales, four barley-malt-based ales (pale, red, Irish, and brown), a stout, and a barley wine. To assist patrons, the back page of the menu lists the beers regularly served arranged from the

With one brewpub in Airdrie, five each in Calgary and Edmonton, and three in Regina, Brewsters is Canada's largest brewpub chain. Pictured above is the Airdrie brewpub, which opened in 2009.

lightest to the darkest, along with notes about the colour, body, flavour characteristics, and ABV of each. To reflect the company's prairie roots, beers are given such names as Wild West Wheat Ale, Farmer's Tan White Ale, Rig Pig Pale Ale, and Bow Valley Brown Ale. One, Lanigan's Irish Ale, reflects the owners' Irish heritage; another, the *hefeweizen*, bears the first name of the Edmonton brewer, Gunther Trageser.

Shortly after he came to Canada in 1987, Trageser began home brewing because he felt the variety of beer available in this country was "terrible." He explained why there were three lagers on the menu: "The Original, which is a premium North American style but with no adjuncts, was our answer to the mainstream lagers available. Flying Frog is more colourful and maltier than Original and has a fuller body. The Czech Pilsner is a more bitter beer in the European tradition. People can progress from the more familiar to the less familiar." He noted that consistency in the menu beers is very important. "They must taste the same each time you try one—in Edmonton or Calgary." But, he remarked with a smile, "It's different with the seasonal brews. I can be more experimental. That's when I become a homebrewer again. I can change my recipes from year to year."

❖

Alberta's other three brewpubs, The Grizzly Paw in Canmore, Jasper Brewing Company in Jasper, and Banff Ave Brewing Company in Banff offer not only good beer and accompanying food, but spectacular views of the Canadian Rockies. In operation since 1996, Grizzly Paw, which was granted a microbrewery licence in 2004, has outlasted three other microbreweries—Bow Valley, Peak, and Canmore Brewworks—in the rapidly growing resort town located a ten-minute drive from the eastern entrance to Banff National Park. Jasper Brewing, established in 2005, enjoys the distinction of being the first brewery to operate within a national park. Banff Ave Brewing, owned by the proprietors of Jasper Brewing, opened in 2010.

The **Grizzly Paw Brewing Company**'s founder, Niall Fraser, who was born in Scotland and began homebrewing in the basement of his family's Edmonton home when he was twelve years old, conceived the idea of opening a brewpub during a stay in Sydney, Australia, where he had become a regular at a local brewpub. Returning to Alberta, he decided to open an establishment in Canmore—it had location (close to the world-famous national park) and it offered spectacular mountain views. The facility has a patio for summer outdoor enjoyment (it's heated for cooler evenings and for fall and winter afternoons) and a large but cosy indoor restaurant and bar with two fireplaces.

Since Grizzly Paw began distributing its beers in bottles and on draft, the cramped brewing facilities have been expanded and three additional fermentation tanks have been placed in an adjacent building. A hose attached to the brewing system's heat exchange unit is run out the door of the brewpub and across an alley to the fermentation tanks. After the brewing is completed, the product is siphoned into tanks on the back of a truck and taken to a nearby warehouse for packaging.

Grizzly Paw initially offered four beer styles, based, Fraser said, on those he had been developing for years in the family basement. Each had a humorous nickname, which often referred to local creatures but with a twist: Grumpy Bear Honey Wheat Ale, Rutting Elk Red, Big Head Nut Brown, and Beaver Tail Raspberry Ale. Grizzly Paw now brews seven beers on a regular basis and rotates a number of seasonals, the most unusual of which was a spruce beer that used evergreen needles.

Michele Lowney, the current brewmaster, is one of a small but growing number of women brewers in North America. A native of Brooklyn, New York, she studied at the Siebel Institute of Brewing in Chicago and worked at a number of breweries (including two in Scotland) before coming to Canmore, attracted by both the professional opportunity and the town's closeness to all-season outdoor activities.

Fraser and Lowney agreed that, if there is a house style characteristic to their beers, it would have to be Scottish. None of them are heavily hopped, as might be the case in a Vancouver Island brewpub. "If we were to follow the styles that are popular in Victoria, Alberta patrons might tell us that the beer is too flat, too warm, or too hoppy," said Fraser. Lowney credits her internship with Williams Brothers Brewery in Scotland for teaching her how to introduce additives so that they enhance the beer. In Grizzly Paw's Grumpy Bear Honey Wheat Ale, honey adds a smoothness and mellowness without an overwhelming sweetness. Ginger Beer, a fall seasonal, uses just enough of the added titular ingredient to provide a hint of the different flavour.

Grizzly Paw's seven menu beers provide a variety of styles to appeal to both the beginning microbrew drinker and the experienced veteran. The 4.5 per cent ABV golden Powder Hound Pilsner has been compared to the more mainstream Kokanee Gold. Brewed in the Czech tradition, with, as the website points out, local "pure glacial water and local pale malts," it has a citrus flavour and slight sweetness. Beaver Tail is an unfiltered wheat ale with tart and sweet flavours imparted by raspberries, while Grumpy Bear uses local honey that creates a floral and sweet taste. Both are 5 per cent beers.

Rutting Elk Red, a medium-bodied Irish ale with caramel overtones, is advertised as "a great introduction to the darker beers. People who want to move beyond our pale beers or have some knowledge will enjoy this classic." At 5.2 per cent ABV, it is, along with Moose Knuckle Oatmeal Stout, Grizzly Paw's strongest brew. Presumably, those who have tried it will graduate to the Indra Island IPA, which is "assertively

Niall Fraser opened Canmore's Grizzly Paw as a brewpub in 1996.
Since then it has been expanded into a microbrewery.

hopped . . . with one hell of a kick," the Big Head Nut Brown Ale, a
medium-bodied ale with caramel and nutty flavours, which has been
named after a Scottish king, and the Oatmeal Stout, the coffee taste of
which comes from beans ground at a Canmore coffee house.

❖

Jasper Brewing Company opened in 2005. "I wanted to return to my
hometown," part owner and original brewmaster Brett Ireland recounted.
He was a recent graduate of the University of Alberta's engineering school,

but because there wasn't much call for his skills in the Rocky Mountain town, he began working in the restaurant business and noticed that tourists frequently asked about local beers—of which there were none. So Ireland, his friends Soc Korogonas and Alex Derksen, and Korogonas's father pooled their resources, successfully applied to the federal government's Small Business Financing Program for a loan, and then opened the first brewpub in a Canadian national park.

After visiting brewpubs in Victoria and Vancouver, they hired Don Moore, a well-known brewing consultant who was then helping set up Fernie Brewery, to assist them. "We went to the Jasper liquor store and bought one each of every kind of beer they had in stock. Then Alex, Soc, and I sat down with Don and discussed styles, colours, and tastes." From ideas that came up at that meeting, they began to develop their menu beers.

Late in the summer of 2005, shortly before Jasper Brewing's opening, the Food Network featured the restaurant and brewpub on its program *Opening Soon*. The program highlighted the spectacular setting—across from the railway station where, for decades, tourists have begun their Jasper vacations. Patrons sitting near the front windows could view not only the station, but the elk that wander the street as though they own it, and the majestic mountains towering beyond the town.

Jasper Brewing offers five core beers, each with a name that links it to the national park. Honey Bear Ale, the top seller, is a 4.8 per cent ABV ale that uses Okanagan Valley honey and coriander, both added during the boil. "It's popular with the people who might like Kokanee," Ireland said. Sutter Hill Pilsner (named after a nearby ski hill) is the second-best seller, a Czech-style beer popular with European visitors. "It's very challenging to make," current brewer Dave Mozel said. "Every step of the way has to be just right. Minerals in the Jasper water change during the year, so we have to tinker with the pH levels for the right kind of softness for a pilsner."

Liftline Cream Ale is based on an English Special Bitter and is infused with nitrogen to give it a creamy head and body. "It's fun," Ireland remarked, "to see our English visitors order a pitcher. They let it sit on the table to warm up, then they drink it and they are thoroughly happy." Rock Hopper IPA, at 5.5 per cent ABV, is the strongest of the core beers and is a heavily hopped West Coast-style ale. "We've increased the

Shortly after graduating from the University of Alberta, Brett Ireland (left) and two friends opened Jasper Brewing Company, the first microbrewery to operate in a Canadian national park. Standing with him is head brewer Dave Mozel.

bitterness levels," Mozel said. "And the pale ale drinkers love it. But then, they're a different breed," he added with a laugh. "But, nobody can top our stout. It's light but flavourful." The 4.4 per cent ABV 6060 Irish-style stout, which is named after the number of an old steam engine on display a few hundred metres from the brewpub, has received high praise from visitors and beer critics alike.

"We respect traditional styles," Ireland said, in discussing the character of their beers. "But we do tinker." Mozel enthusiastically added, "Brewing is an art with serendipity. I enjoy playing around to hit the right combination." He made three trial runs until he got the Blueberry Vanilla Ale, a summer seasonal, the way he wanted it. Blueberry-infused beers are not uncommon, but the vanilla beans add a unique variation.

Encouraged by the success of the Jasper operation, Ireland, Korogonas, and a new partner, Dan Rodrigues, opened a second brewpub. In June 2010,

Banff Ave Brewing Company became the first company to legally brew beer in Canada's most famous national park. (Earlier breweries with similar names, Banff Brewery and Banff Brewing Company, had operated out of Calgary and Edmonton, respectively.) "We'd be dealing with similar market demographics as Jasper—world travellers, Canadian vacationers, and locals—but on a much bigger scale. Somebody once described Banff as Jasper on steroids," Ireland said. Although there was the usual paperwork to wade through, it was easier the second time around. "We'd had the experience of dealing with the various kinds of government paperwork, we'd set a precedent for national parks, and we had a track record."

They located the new brewery on the second floor of the Clock Tower Building, an Austrian alpine-style structure that housed other tourist businesses, including an RCMP souvenir store. With a seating capacity of two hundred and seventy-five, the brewpub was much larger than the one in Jasper; it wasn't divided into a restaurant and bar, but was designed as a pub lounge, with couches and low tables. And it had a summer patio, something lacking in the Jasper operation. "It faces west," Ireland noted, "so people will have fabulous views of the mountains and sunsets." The menu is similar to that at Jasper, "only slightly more upscale."

"The biggest challenge was the water; it's much harder than Jasper's. That meant we had to tinker with our beer recipes to get them just right. Our beer list will be the same, but it may taste a little different. Of course, we called in Don Moore to help us in the brewery."

Not only will the beers taste a little different, they'll have different names. "When we were in Jasper, the local people were really proud of us. We were the town's brewery. We want the people of Banff to be proud of their first brewery. We've got them involved in naming the beers." So the mild blonde ale is called Banff Ave, the Czech-style pilsner is Czuggers, the IPA is Head Smashed, the cream ale (described as being like an ESB) is Brewer's Oar, the stout is Reverend Rundle, and the black pilsner is Lower Bankhead. There's also a summer seasonal—Stubble Jumper Saskatoon Berry Ale.

Big Rock Brewery
    5555 76th Ave SE, Calgary, T2C 4L8, 403-720-3239, bigrockbeer.com
Brew Brothers Brewery
    607 11th Ave SW, Calgary, T2R 0E1, 403-258-2739, brewbrothers.com

Wild Rose Brewery

    2 - 4580 Quesnay Wood Dr SW, Calgary, T3E 7J3, 403-720-2733

    wildrosebrewery.com

Brewsters Brewing Company and Restaurant, brewsters.ca

    11th Avenue

        834 11th Ave, Calgary, T2R 0E5, 403-265-2739

    Airdrie

        200 - 3 Stonegate Dr NW, Airdrie, T4B 0N2, 403-945-2739

    Crowfoot

        25 Crowfoot Terr NW, Calgary, T3G 4J8, 403-208-2739

    Foothills

        4419 53rd St SE, Calgary, T2C 4V1

    Lake Bonavista

        176 - 755 Lake Bonavista Dr SW, Calgary, T2J 0N3, 403-225-2739

    Mckenzie Towne

        100 - 11 Mckenzie Towne Blvd SE, Calgary, T2Z 0S8, 403-243-2739

The Grizzly Paw Brewing Company

    622 8th St, Canmore, T1W 2B5 , 403-678-9983, thegrizzlypaw.com

Jasper Brewing Company

    624 Connaught Dr, Jasper, T0E 1E0, 780-852-4111, jasperbrewingco.ca

Banff Ave Brewing Company

    110 Banff Ave, Banff, T1L 1G2, 403-762-1003, banffbrewingco.ca

The British Co
and the Yukon

Part Two

The British Columbia Interior and the Yukon

Between 1861, when the short-lived Lillooet Brewery opened, and 1917, when Prohibition was imposed on British Columbians, twenty-eight interior communities, from Natal in the southeast to Atlin in the northwest, hosted breweries. Many of them came and went as quickly as the foam cresting a glass of bad beer, victims of the economic misfortunes of the boom towns in which they were built. Only four of the breweries operating in 1917 returned after the end of Prohibition in 1920.

In 1950, the Fernie Brewing Company, the Cranbrook Brewing Company, and the Kootenay Brewing Company plants in Trail and Nelson formed the Interior Brewing Consortium, which, a decade later, moved all brewing operations to Creston, where it operated as the Interior Brewing Company. In 1972, Labatt purchased the company and changed its name to Columbia Brewing Company. It still operates in Creston as Columbia Brewery. In 1955, the Nechako Brewing Company opened in Prince George, operated with many owners and under a variety of names, and survived into the twenty-first century as Pacific Western Brewing.

The microbrewing revolution arrived in the interior in 1985, when Okanagan Spring of Vernon sold its first keg of beer. Since then, twenty microbreweries or brewpubs have operated from Fernie to Smithers. In the summer of 2010, sixteen of them were still open. In 1997, the first Yukon brewery in over a century opened in Whitehorse.

New Brews in Old Beer Towns
Fernie to Nelson

In 1960, when the beer bearing its name began being brewed in Creston, the town of Fernie was in an economic slump. But by 2002, when the new **Fernie Brewing Company** began to sell its pale ale to local taverns, the economic situation had improved greatly. High-grade coal was in demand from steel plants overseas, and the area had become a popular four-season vacation destination. Undeterred by recent failures of microbreweries in nearby Kimberley and Windermere, father and son Russell and Murray Pask decided to create a microbrewery. They began expanding and renovating a garage on the family's ranch so that it could accommodate a ten-hectolitre brewing system. Most important, they hired Don Moore, a respected western Canadian brewer who had assisted in the start-up of breweries in British Columbia and Alberta.

"The important thing," Moore recalled several years later, "was to create quality beers that wouldn't be too different from the ones people were used to, but that had a certain distinctiveness." The first product, a pale ale, drew on consumers' familiarity with Okanagan Spring's popular pale ale. "It was designed to be a crossover beer," Murray Pask commented. "It was a 'not-too' beer: not too hoppy, not too dark, and not too full-bodied." Their second beer, an English brown ale that was similar to Alberta's Big Rock Traditional Ale, was designed to appeal to Calgary visitors, while their third, a lager, aimed at winning a section of the market from the very popular Kokanee lager. For two years the brews were available, on draft and in one-litre plastic and then glass bottles, from Cranbrook in the west to Windermere in the north. With the introduction of cans in 2005, sales grew threefold and the remodelled garage became too small to handle the increased volume. In 2007, Fernie Brewing moved off the ranch to the edge of town, to a state-of-the-art modern brewery that now produces three thousand hectolitres of beer annually.

Brewer Warren Smith, who began his career at Calgary's Wild Rose Brewery, started a description of the five beers Fernie Brewing produces

With the popularity of Fernie Brewing's beers growing rapidly, Russell and Murray Pask moved brewing operations from a garage on the family ranch to a state-of-the-art facility at the edge of Fernie.

by saying, "We want all our beers to be session beers," that is, not too high in alcohol content (none are over 5 per cent ABV), and smooth, flavourful, and easy to drink. "At first, The Griz Pale Ale was too much like an India Pale Ale, so we pulled out a lot of the hops, making it more like a Special Old Bitter." First Trax Brown Ale was created "to be a celebration of malt. We use eleven different malts in our recipe. There's a roasty taste and a medium body that people like. Our new lager, Rocky Mountain Genuine Lager, moves away from the mainstream. We wanted it to be more like a continental pilsner than a North American lager."

With a spectrum of beers from blonde to amber to brown firmly established, Fernie Brewing branched out into two styles that are becoming increasingly popular: *wit* beer and fruit beer. Ol' Willy Wit (named after the town's founder, William Fernie) is an unfiltered wheat beer with a bready taste and chewy texture. At first, some Bud drinkers balked at the new brew, remarking of the unfiltered yeast: "Something is in my beer." But Ol' Willy is gradually gaining converts. What the Huck, a lighter-coloured wheat beer, is flavoured with huckleberries that grow wild in the eastern Kootenays. "Our first batch, which used locally picked berries, sold out in two weeks," Smith said, "but it's very labour intensive to pick them and they can't be domesticated, so we now depend on an extract." Both brews were introduced as seasonal offerings, but are now available all year on draft and in 650-millilitre bottles.

Looking at the results of their first seven years in business, Pask and Smith explained the successes of Fernie Brewing. "We resisted the pressures to become more mainstream," Smith remarked, "and produced a quality product that would introduce our customers to styles that were different but not threatening." Pask spoke of the local support the beers have received. "We wanted something that would please the locals, as well as the tourists, and that would travel beyond the immediate area."

❖

When the Interior Brewing plant opened in Creston at the end 1959, it was local or at least regional. When the mayor of Nelson suggested that the brewery name a beer after the nearby Kokanee Glacier, the connection with southeastern BC was strengthened. After Labatt bought the brewery in 1972 and named it **Columbia Brewery**, it was still a local business—Kokanee, its best-selling beer, wasn't available throughout BC until 1985. But when Labatt closed its New Westminster plant in 2005, the Creston brewery became the third-largest producer of beer west of London, Ontario.

The company encourages people to consider the brewery a local producer situated in a pristine natural area. There are references to a "glacier-fresh" product, to "a small mountain brewery," and to a lineage reaching back to 1898, when a brewery at Fort Steele moved to Fernie. Labels show snow-capped mountains, and humorous commercials suggest a small-town operation near a wilderness where beer-stealing sasquatches and portals to alternate universes may be found.

If the more than ten thousand people who annually tour Columbia Brewery expect to see a small, quaint production facility, they will be surprised. There *is* a sasquatch near the gates to the brewery, but it's a forty-thousand-dollar statue of the mythic creature moving through the trees, clutching a case of Kokanee under its arm. Inside the brewery, which employs a hundred and fifty people, visitors see state-of-the-art,

This statue of a sasquatch stealing a case of Kokanee
beer stands in front of Columbia Brewery in Creston.

computer-co-ordinated brewing equipment capable of turning out one
million cans of beer a day on a twenty-million-dollar canning line.

The old Kokanee advertising slogan—"It's the beer out here"—still
holds. Kokanee remains the top-selling beer in BC and, until 2007, was
also the best seller in Alberta. All the Kokanee consumed in Canada
and in several northwestern states comes from here and so do all Labatt
products sold in BC, including the very popular value-priced Lucky
Lager. Since the late summer of 2009, the plant has also brewed Labatt's
Halifax-based Alexander Keith's IPA and Red for western Canada.

Kokanee is a mainstream North American lager, 5 per cent ABV, pale
yellow in colour and very lightly hopped. Kokanee Gold, at 5.3 per cent
ABV, is slightly fuller bodied and has a maltier flavour. Kokanee Light is
a 4 per cent ABV beer. A fourth product, Kootenay True Ale, is slightly
hoppier, darker in colour, and fuller in malt taste. It is brewed to provide
an alternative beer for people in the Kootenays.

One of Creston's biggest employers, Columbia Brewery inspires fierce
loyalty among many townspeople, who either don't realize or don't care

that it is part of the international Anheuser-Busch InBev conglomerate. It is, to Crestonites, "our brewery," a fact that was made clear in the fall of 2009 when the local newspaper carried a report that Miller-Coors, part of another multinational, was threatening legal action because the mountains depicted on the Kokanee labels were too similar to those used on Coors products. The townspeople were indignant and spoke angrily in defense of their "local" company.

❖❖

To travel from Columbia Brewery in Creston to **Nelson Brewing Company** involves a slow, winding, and very scenic seventy-eight-kilometre drive along the eastern shore of Kootenay Lake, a fifteen-minute ferry ride across the lake, and a thirty-five-kilometre drive into a city that isn't much larger than Creston. Midway across the lake, ferry passengers move from the Mountain to the Pacific time zone. But the trip involves more than making an adjustment to one's watch. In a real sense, travelling from a brewery that produces 1.3 million hectolitres of beer a year to one producing just over six thousand means moving into a totally different brewing world, from high-tech to handcrafted.

The brewery is away from the centre of Nelson, on a tree-lined street only two blocks from a fire hall made famous by the Steve Martin movie *Roxanne*. It's housed in the second-oldest commercially used building in the city, which, from the 1890s until the late 1950s, had housed another brewery. It shares the building with a tofu maker, a guitar manufacturer, a mountain bike distributor, and a coffee-roasting company.

"Deiter Feist and Paddy Glenny [who founded the brewery in 1991] chose Nelson because the local liquor stores sold more imported and microbrewed beers per capita than anywhere else in BC," managing partner Tim Pollock said. "In fact, per capita sales of Okanagan Spring products were higher here than in Vernon [that brewery's location]. To establish a connection with the earlier brewery, Feist and Glenny decided to locate in the old brewery and to resurrect its name. Our logo is the same as the old one."

The brewery began operations just as Columbia Brewery started its expansion eastward across Canada. Not surprisingly, going up against

Brewmaster Mike Kelly adds organic BC honey to
Nelson Brewing Company's Wild Honey Organic Ale.

Kokanee, "the beer out here," represented Nelson Brewing's biggest challenge. Old Brewery Pale Ale and Silver King Lager were Nelson's first offerings. "We found that the local market didn't want a microbrewed lager so we dropped Silver King and decided that we'd primarily be an ale house. Old Brewery Pale Ale is still one of our most popular offerings."

Nelson's citizenry soon embraced the new brewery. "Without the support of the people in Nelson and within an eighty-kilometre radius, we wouldn't be here." When Feist and Glenny decided to withdraw from the business, Pollock strengthened Nelson Brewing's local roots, recruiting three prominent Nelson businessmen as major investors.

After nearly two decades, Nelson Brewing's annual production of just over six thousand hectolitres is only .5 per cent of the annual production of its Creston neighbour, but the brewery has grown. Available at first only on draft, the beer was later packaged in one litre-bottles, then in 341-millilitre bottles, and, since 2006, also in 355-millilitre cans. It is now distributed to liquor stores all around the province and to select Alberta locations.

The biggest change in the brewery occurred in 2006, when its products received organic certification. "The microbrewing industry had become increasingly crowded," Pollock commented. "We felt that going organic would enhance the quality of our beers and that Nelson was certainly the kind of place where offering organic beer would sell. Mike Kelly, our brewer, did the legwork. The challenge was to keep the beer profiles similar while using organic materials." Kelly purchased organic malt from Gambrinus Malting in Armstrong, just north of Vernon. It was more difficult to find organic hops, and the search extended to Belgium and New Zealand. "But we're trying to encourage local farmers to grow organic hops." In fact, one of the dreams of the brewery is for all of its ingredients to come from within eight hundred kilometres of Nelson. A slogan on the bottle caps reflects Nelson Brewing's pride in both its organic product and its role in the area: "The natural choice of the Kootenays."

Mike Kelly, who studied at the prestigious University of California, Davis, brewing school and worked at High Mountain Brewpub in Whistler and Howe Sound Brewpub in Squamish before coming to Nelson, described the various beers he brews. Common to all of them, he emphasized, is an adherence to the characteristics of classic styles, with some tweaking. "I want my beers to be clean and balanced—a person should be able to taste all the flavours. In a way, you could say I want my beers to be both simple and subtle." The beers range in strength from 4.5 per cent ABV (Wild Honey Ale and Liplock Summer Ale) to

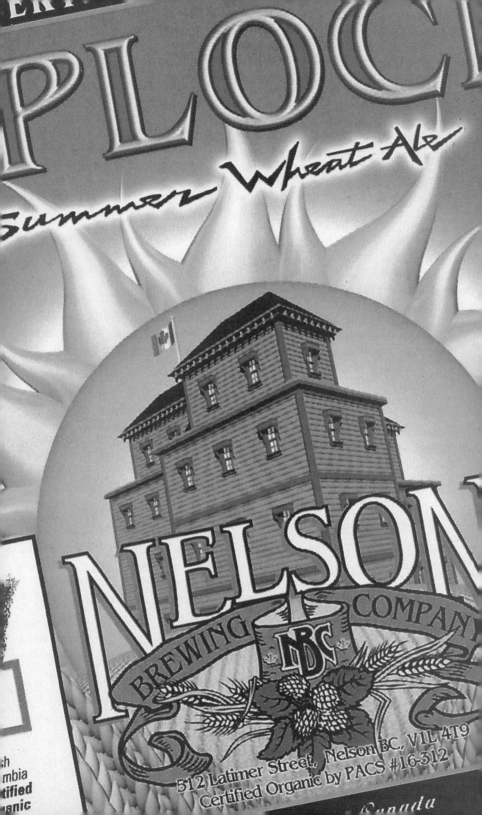

6.5 per cent (Paddywhack IPA and Faceplant Winter Ale), and in colour from pale gold (Liplock) to dark brown (After Dark and Faceplant).

Four of the ales are at the lighter end of the spectrum. Liplock, a summer release, is an unfiltered *hefeweizen*, a wheat beer that, he said is, "like the smell of fresh baked bread." Wild Honey Organic Ale introduces local wild honey during the boil to provide a subtle, not too sweet flavour. Old Brewery Pale Ale (which has won both a silver and a bronze at the Canadian Brewing Awards) achieves a balance of hops and malts. Kelly commented on its nuanced aromas and recommended that before quaffing, people should stick their noses in the glass and really sniff. Paddywhack IPA is, according to the advertising copy, "heavenly hopped to the edge." However, the hops are not overwhelming, as the malts create a balance of flavours. It has won a Canadian Brewing Awards gold medal.

After Dark, an English-style dark mild ale (5 per cent ABV) is lower on hops than the two pale ales and is, Kelly said, a smooth, creamy, easy-drinking ale. Blackheart Oatmeal Stout (5.7 per cent ABV), which has also won a Canadian Brewing Awards gold medal, has small amounts of oatmeal added during the mashing stage to create a silky, creamy mouth-feel. Faceplant Winter Ale emphasizes the malt along with brown sugar and molasses.

Fernie Brewing Company
    25 Manitou Rd, Fernie, V0M 1M5, 250-423-7733, ferniebrewing.com
Columbia Brewery
    1220 Erickson St, Creston, V0B 1G0, 250-428-1228, columbiabrewery.com
Nelson Brewing Company
    412 Latimer St, Nelson, V1L 4T9, 250-352-3582, nelsonbrewing.com

CHAPTER FOUR

Not Just About the Wine
The Okanagan Valley

The Okanagan Valley, stretching from the United States border to north of Vernon, is justly renowned for its wineries—seventy-one of them, according to a 2009 tourist brochure. But during the summer and early fall of that year, drivers along Highway 97 from Osoyoos to Kamloops would have noticed, in addition to signs pointing to nearby wineries, several large billboards announcing "You're in Pil Country." Behind the words were enlargements of parts of the label for Old Style pilsner beer.

Originally brewed at Sick's Lethbridge brewery and later at its plant in Vancouver, the beer has been brewed since 1958 by Molson. Since Molson closed the Lethbridge facility in 1989, it has been produced only in Vancouver. The intention of the billboard advertising campaign seems to have been to boost sales of what is, in the west, one of the company's important value-priced brands. The area really isn't "Pil Country," although the ads hope to make it so.

That is not to say that the Okanagan Valley isn't *beer* country. From Osoyoos to Armstrong, just north of Vernon, there are three brewpubs, three microbreweries, a regional brewery, and a branch of an international brewing company. Among them, the eight breweries regularly produce forty-seven different beers, ten of them lagers, one of which is a pilsner. The valley is currently more pale ale, brown ale, and fruit beer country than Pil Country.

Vernon, at the north end of Okanagan Lake, was home to two short-lived breweries in the late nineteenth century, and Kelowna, halfway down the lake, to one shortly before the Second World War. When Okanagan Spring began operations in Vernon in 1985, it was the region's first brewery in nearly a half century. Then, between 1995 and 2000, four microbreweries—three of which are still operating—sprang up in Kelowna and Penticton. In 1993, Granville Island Brewing, which had grown from a microbrewery to a regional brewery, established its main production facility in Kelowna.

Stefan Tobler, brewmaster and son of one of the founders of Okanagan Spring Brewery, stands in front of kegs stacked in the warehouse of the brewery, which began as a micro-brewery in 1985 and is now part of Sapporo of Japan's international brewing empire.

When **Jakob Tobler** and Buko von Krosigk founded **Okanagan Spring Brewery,** they had no idea that within a quarter of a century it would

PALE A[LE]

Brewed by Okanagan Spring in 198[9]
[Th]is is BC's original & favourite Pale A[le]

[Cl]ear and copper coloured, it is fruity on the palate a[nd]
[he]arty in hops with a nice, round finish. We are honour[ed]
[th]at Pale Ale continues to be BC's most popular craft br[ew]

BREWMASTER STEFAN TOBLE[R]

FIRST BREWED IN BC
89

Colour Scale

9

COPPER

50% alc/vol

ENJOYED BEST AT

9-11°C

The craft of making a true Pale Ale

The taste and quality of our Pale Ale is what we mean when we say "craft-brewed". Inspired by beer lovers, we use the best ingredients, longer brewing times and exacting care during each step of the process.

NATURAL
[P]RESERVATIVES
[PASTEU]RIZED

341 mL

BEER / BIÈRE   PRODUCT OF CANADA / PRO[DUIT]
CRAFT-BREWED BY OKANAGAN SPRING V[ERNON]

be part of a multinational brewing company. Tobler, a restaurateur, and von Krosigk, a real estate developer, wanted to provide local residents and summer tourists with the kind of beer they had enjoyed growing up in Germany: all natural, with no adjuncts. However, after the first year, when they produced thirty-seven hundred hectolitres of beer and lost half a million dollars, they realized that they would also have to distribute their beers in the Lower Mainland and on Vancouver Island if they were to survive. They increased production at their Vernon plant and, within eight years, volume had risen to sixty thousand hectolitres a year.

In 1995, the original shareholders were bought out by Allied Strategies, which, in turn, was bought out a year later by Sleeman Brewery of Ontario, which was then at the beginning of an expansion program designed to transform it from a regional to a national brewery. Then, in 2006, Sapporo of Japan purchased Sleeman.

By 2010, Okanagan Spring was producing over three hundred and seventy-thousand hectolitres annually and employing a hundred and twenty people. In addition to its own brands, it brews three styles of Shaftebury (an early BC microbrewery and another Sleeman acquisition), selected Sleeman brands and Old Milwaukee, Rainier, Blue Ribbon, Colt 45, and Strohs, all value-priced American beers, for the western Canadian market. It's ironic that there is still a small sign at the edge of town that reads "Craft Brewery" and has an arrow pointing toward the very large facility.

Okanagan Spring's current brewmaster, Stefan Tobler, the son of one of the founders and an employee since the brewery's early years, came by the trade naturally. He grew up in Bavaria, an area famous for its breweries, five or six of which, he has noted, are within ten kilometres of his old home. After joining his family in Vernon and working at the brewery, he returned to Germany to complete an apprenticeship and later a master's certification in brewing.

Back in Vernon, he helped create Okanagan Spring's original beer, a premium lager, brewed according to the German purity law of 1516, and then developed Extra Special Pale Ale, one of British Columbia's first examples of that style. It quickly became the company's best seller and one of the most popular beers in the province. "We wanted to try something different," Tobler explained. "But we didn't want to overwhelm people." He avoided the often-assertive hoppiness of many pale ales. Although the label says that it is "hearty in hops," malts dominate.

Proud as he is of the pale ale, Tobler stated, "I like my lagers." 1516 Bavarian Lager, his own creation, is light-bodied and crisp, with noticeable hoppiness. "It was designed to bring mainstream drinkers slowly over to beer in the German tradition." Tobler's most recent creation, Brewmaster's Black Lager, features dark and chocolate malts, but is light-bodied, clean and crisp. "There was some initial resistance to the colour, but since then the response has been very positive." There was also a quick response from Molson, which felt that the original title, Black Lager, was too close to its own value-priced brand, Black Label. The word "Brewmaster's" was added to placate the multinational brewer.

Speaking of his beers, Tobler emphasized the importance of consistency of taste—something which is, he says, hard to get. "When I drink a beer, it needs to tell me, 'Yes, you want another.' Then I know it's good." Drinkability, he feels, is crucial. This suggests why the Okanagan Spring beers are flavourful, but not too assertive, and why the brewery's products are among the most popular in BC.

❖

At about the time that Sleeman Brewery was casting covetous eyes at Okanagan Spring, Geoff Twyman, a one-time homebrewer and former assistant winemaker at Kelowna's Cedar Crest Winery, was planning to opening a microbrewery in Kelowna. His plans came to fruition on April 29, 1996, when **Tree Brewing Company** offered Amber Ale to the drinking public. A blonde lager, a red ale, and a dark lager followed. When the brewery celebrated its tenth anniversary, only the Amber Ale remained on its list.

Although the brewery expanded fairly rapidly, reaching a respectable annual production of seventy-five hundred hectolitres, the expansion came at a considerable cost. To meet the greater expenses, Twyman sold shares in the company, but Tree had to be rescued from bankruptcy twice, by Clearly Canadian Beverage in 2000 and by a group of Calgary investors led by Wayne Clements in 2003. The new investors concentrated on quality, rather than on quantity, and rebranded the products. Amber

Tree Brewing's brewmaster Stefan Buhl and CEO Tod Melnyk
enjoy one of the Kelowna brewery's award-winning beers as
they stand in front of a shelf displaying many of the awards.

became Thirsty Beaver, a name that, among other things, suggested the
Canadian outdoors. The pale ale became Cutthroat Pale Ale, another
reference to outdoor life. The group also adopted the general slogan
"Beer with Character for People with Character." Sales grew steadily.

Tod Melnyk, who, after eighteen years with Labatt, became Tree's
CEO in 2007, attributed the company's growth to employing good
people, brewing good products, and spending money wisely. "You can't
go head-to-head against the big guys with their huge advertising budgets. You have to educate people that there are beers that have much
more flavour than the mainstream lagers. We do, however, get attention
with the humorous names of our products. We take the beer seriously,
but not ourselves. We are working to push people's taste boundaries and
to get them thinking about beer in the same way as many of them think
about wine—that there are different beers for different times and different foods. We don't rigidly follow style guidelines; we push boundaries
when we make our beers."

Stefan Buhl, who, like Okanagan Spring's Stefan Tobler, received his training in Germany, came to Canada in 1996 to work for Peak Brewery in Canmore, Alberta, and moved to Kelowna in 2000 when Peak's parent company purchased Tree. Talking about styles, he remarked, "I believe that 1516 gives people more than enough options." He was referring to the *Reinheitsgebot*, the German purity law that restricted the ingredients of beer to water, malted grain, hops, and yeast. "There is so much variety in the four ingredients that there are many combinations and style variations available."

Typical of microbreweries, Tree has five regular offerings that span the colour spectrum, from the light Kelowna Pilsner to the dark Spy Porter. The pilsner is designed as an entry beer for those used to drinking mainstream lagers. "But," Melnyk remarked, "if you make a lager, make it different." Buhl introduced more malty flavours than the mainstream parallels, used Saaz hops to produce a clean flavour like that of the German beers he had learned about during his schooling, and made sure the beer had a longer aging period to enhance the crisp finish. The name, certainly the tamest in the Tree line, was an attempt to get more Kelowna people to embrace Tree's products. Paradoxically, Kelowna has been the slowest of Tree's markets, which extend from Victoria to Winnipeg. The pilsner won a silver medal in the 2007 Canadian Brewing Awards.

Like Nelson Brewing, Tree brews two pale ales. Cutthroat Pale Ale balances five different types of hops against five different malts and emphasizes hop aroma, but not bitterness. With only twenty IBUs, it is designed for those who like lighter beers that have more nuanced hop flavours and aromas. By contrast, Hophead India Pale Ale, Tree's best-selling bottled beer, is bitter—all sixty IBUs of it. "But," Buhl emphasized, "there is a balance between the hops and malts." The former beer won a Canadian Brewing Awards gold medal in 2007, the latter a bronze that year and a silver the next.

After fifteen years, Thirsty Beaver Amber remains the workhorse of the list: Tree's overall best-selling beer. A smooth, English-style amber beer, it reaches Buhl's stated goal of creating something everyone can drink. The dark malts give a full-bodied mouth-feel with just a slight bitterness. "With the mixture of malts, every palate tastes something."

Rounding out the offerings is Spy Porter, which started out as a dark lager and then evolved into a porter using chocolate malts. It is medium-bodied, and has roasted and toasted notes, and a clean finish

Tree also creates seasonal beers and what the brewers call "Occasional Rarities." The most successful seasonal is their Hefeweizen, a German-style beer that uses traditional yeasts to give the finished brew a banana-clove flavour. It received a Canadian Brewing Awards gold medal in 2008 and a silver in 2009. Hophead Double Imperial Pale Ale is 8 per cent ABV. One of the Occasional Rarities, it was a 2009 gold medal winner at the Canadian Brewing Awards. During the fall of 2009, Buhl created Black Tree, a mix of porter and pale ale. For each bottle sold, the company planned to finance the planting of one tree to replace trees lost during that summer's forest fires.

❖

Next door to Tree Brewing's Richter Street headquarters is a large building housing the main brewing and packaging facilities of **Granville Island Brewing**. There is still a boutique brewery on Vancouver's Granville Island but in 1993, Potter Distilling, which had purchased the brewery in 1989, moved its operations to Kelowna, to the building it shared with the company's wine-making division. Taken over in 2005 by Andrew Peller, another winery, the brewery was sold in the fall of 2009 to Creemore Springs Brewery, itself owned by Molson, part of the international conglomerate that includes Molson, Miller, Coors, and South African Breweries. Like Okanagan Spring, founded a year after Granville Island, Canada's first microbrewery had grown far beyond its local, "cottage brewery" beginnings. (A discussion of Granville Island's beers is found on pages 153–157).

❖

Three of the brewpubs operating in the interior of BC are located along Highway 97 between Osoyoos and Kelowna. In an area where products of Columbia and Okanagan Spring, the interior's largest brewers, dominate draft sales, each of the three brewpubs has worked to educate its customers on the difference between the beverages created by the large brewers and those made by brewpubs.

Freddy's Brewpub and Mill Creek Brewing is on the north side of Kelowna, on what, until the early 1990s, was the site of Flintstone Amusement Park. Unlike Ridge Brew House in Osoyoos and Barley Mill Pub in Penticton, which are hard to miss, Freddy's is easy to drive past. It's set well back from Highway 97 in a mall that includes a movie complex, a family exercise centre, and a bowling alley. The location no doubt explains why most of the restaurant-pub's customers are local, people who have come for dinner and a beer or for a pre- or post-movie snack. "The summer is our least busy season. Tourists are welcome, but it's mainly local people," said manager Michael Mitchell. "When fall bowling leagues begin and the holiday party season approaches, we get very busy."

The laminated placemats that describe the five in-house draft beers include terms such as "lightest," "light but full of flavour," "moderately hopped," and "lighter than it looks." Brewer Jack Clark, who retired to Kelowna after a thirty-year career as brewer and plant manager for Labatt operations across Canada, described the challenge of developing products for Freddy's. "I like beer with lots of hop and malt flavours, really dark ales and IPAs. But that just doesn't work in Kelowna. People want things to be different, but not too different. Quite a few people were reluctant to try our brown ale. And I would never do an IPA—it just wouldn't sell. I tried a Scottish ale and a Vienna lager. The people who liked them were very positive but there weren't enough people to justify brewing them again."

Back Country Lager, the top seller, is a clear, crisp lager designed, Clark said, "to offer a choice for those who liked domestic lagers [his term for products from megabrewers]. It's lightly hopped and doesn't have a pronounced flavour profile." The slightly more challenging Red Head Lager uses a variety of malts and more hops. The malty character, particularly that contributed by the caramel malts, distinguishes it from Back Country Lager. Designed as a crossover beer, it is, surprisingly, often passed over by customers when the tanks containing Back Country run dry.

"People usually jump from the Back Country to the Honey Ridge Ale. Like most honey beers, its honey is mainly in name. The dominant characteristic is supplied by the coriander. We add four pounds of it to

killer bee
(dark honey ale)

THE TIN WHISTLE

BREWING COMPANY

KETTLE VALLEY LINE no 1 1901

vol.

rong Beer / Bière Fort

onsibly.

oney Ale / Biere Anglaise Foncee de Miel

r

, Malt, Yeast, Hops

each batch to provide spicy and citrus attributes," Clark said. Honey Ridge places a close second to Back Country as the brewpub's most popular beer.

As the name suggests, Lord Nelson's Pale Ale is an English-style beer. The most heavily hopped of Freddy's beers, it is, Mitchell remarked, "a tough sell to the Budweiser-Kokanee crowd but European visitors love it." Heavy hopping in this case is relative, for it is moderately hopped. The Cascade hops provide a citrus-grapefruit note. "But," Clark stressed, "it isn't bitter."

Brownstone Ale rounds out the roster of beers. Although it is a traditional English brown ale, it is, to repeat the advertising copy, "lighter than it looks." Brewed with several malts, it depends on a small amount of chocolate malt to give it its colour and a nutty, roasted flavour. "It's a steady seller," said Mitchell. "Our customers like the fact that it is mild and has no bitterness." It is, as Clark said of all his brews, "different, but not too different."

❖

Penticton's two microbreweries, Tin Whistle Brewing Company, established in 1995, and Cannery Brewing Company, founded in 2001, have several things in common. Each is run by people from the restaurant business, each is in a historical building, and each has achieved success not only by brewing good beer, but also by learning how to navigate BC's labyrinthine and, some would say, draconian liquor laws.

Three years after **Tin Whistle Brewing Company** began operations, its first owners, Linda and Richard Grierson and Lawrie and Lynda Lock, ran into financial difficulties, and Lorraine Nagy, who had been part owner of a local hotel and restaurant, purchased the company. "I ran the beer and wine store at the hotel," she explained. "But when my partners decided to sell, it was too early for me to retire. Tin Whistle became available, and buying it seemed like a good idea." But she soon learned that making beer and selling it to retailers were very different from selling it to consumers. "It was a steep learning curve. I had to learn about suppliers, the whole brewing process, and BC's liquor laws— which were something else." She also wanted people to realize that beer wasn't just a generic "poor man's" drink. Like wines, there were many

Lorraine Nagy, owner of Tin Whistle Brewing,
watches as brewer Jeff Todd adds water to the mash tun.

styles, with different tastes and mouth-feels. "I wanted our restaurant customers to realize that, like wine, different beers could be paired with different foods."

One of her first acts after acquiring Tin Whistle (which was the name of a steam locomotive on the Kettle Valley Railroad, a long-ago line that ran out of Penticton), was to instruct her brewmaster to tinker with the brewery's original recipes. "I wanted to blend my personal tastes with customer demand." Rattle Snake ESB was retired, both because it wasn't selling well enough and because Nagy and most customers didn't like its strong hop bitterness and flavours. Coyote was transformed from a pale ale into a milder blonde ale. Peaches and Cream, a peach-apricot-flavoured brew, became Peach Cream Ale. "Overall," she said, "we lightened the beers."

Tin Whistle's current brewer is Jeff Todd, a former history and classical studies major at the University of Victoria, who discovered that he enjoyed experiencing Victoria's microbrew culture more than studying ancient cultures. After graduation, he took what he referred to as a crash course in brewing from retiring Tin Whistle brewer Ron Bradley. Recently, walking around the kettles, tuns, and tanks housed in what used to be a small museum, he discussed the company's six beers.

Centennial, the new name for the altered Coyote beer, is gold in colour, with neither hops nor malts dominating. "It's designed to be our session beer," Todd explained. "We add 10 per cent wheat to give it a rich and creamy finish." Kettle Valley Amber is "designed to be our gateway beer, a darker ale with more complex malt flavours. People who start with Centennial can enjoy Kettle Valley and then move on to our brown ale and porter." Medium amber, it has a mild chocolate-coffee taste.

Both Nagy and Todd waxed poetic when asked to describe Peach Cream Ale. "It represents the Okanagan; it's a happy beer," enthused Nagy. "It's the Okanagan in a bottle!" Todd said. A lighter version of its predecessor, Peaches and Cream, it has a hoppy bite and a hint of peach. Its name suggests not only the area's main agricultural product, but also the beer's smooth finish. "One of the reasons we changed the name from Peaches and Cream," Todd added, "is that people thought that it referred to a type of corn, and we didn't want them to think we used adjuncts in our beer."

In spite of its aggressive, threatening name, Black Widow is a mild brown English ale. It is relatively full-flavoured, but not overpowering, and, like Tin Whistle's other beers, it is very smooth, with no harsh aftertaste. "When people see the rich brown head they think it's like Guinness. But it's not; it's not threatening at all."

Tin Whistle's other two beers are more assertive. Killer Bee Dark Honey Ale, made with dark wildflower honey, is 6 per cent ABV, 1 per cent more than the other five beers. Dark brown, it has a coffee taste, the edge of which is taken away by a hint of the honey. "It makes you want to lick your lips," Todd laughed. Chocolate Cherry Porter is what Todd called "our robust beer." It's a full-bodied drink in which the sweetness of the cherries balances the slight bitterness of the Belgian-style dark chocolate. "Our chocolate," he proudly announced, "is made by the brother of Bernard Callebaut [the world-renowned Calgary chocolate maker]."

While Jeff Todd described the beers, Lorraine Nagy not only added her own comments, but emphasized that she didn't feel that her products were in direct competition with other Okanagan brewers, particularly

Patt Dyck, along with her husband, Ron, founded Cannery Brewing
after nearly a quarter of a century in the restaurant business.

Cannery Brewing, less than two kilometres away. "We offer an alternative," she stressed, noting Tin Whistle's success in creating beers with fruit and such other additives as chocolate and honey. She summed up her philosophy, "There's a beer for everyone; you just have to find it."

After operating a restaurant in nearby Naramata for twenty-three years, Ron and Patt Dyck, the owners of **Cannery Brewing Company**, decided that the business was better suited to younger people. When their chef, Terry Schoffer, an enthusiastic homebrewer, discovered some commercial brewing equipment for sale, the three decided to start a new business. Like Lorraine Nagy, they set up shop in a historic Penticton building, the Aylmer Fruit and Vegetable Company's former canning plant, which had the kind of plumbing and drainage systems essential for a brewery. The brewery, which has been expanded, shares the building with a saddlery, commercial baker's retail outlet, yoga studio, belly dance studio, and New Age gift shop.

The company introduced its products on April Fool's Day, 2001, with the launch of Naramata Nut Brown Ale, still its best-selling brew. "We didn't want to create a mainstream beer because it would cost too much money to go against the major brewers," Patt remembered. "We wanted to fill a void and create a long-ago favourite that wasn't easily available in the Okanagan. At first, people were a little leery, but we operated with the philosophy 'If you try it, you'll like it' and had a lot of tastings in the Okanagan. It sold itself, and it still does."

At first, Cannery's beers were available only on draft and in plastic, refillable party pigs. However, as demand increased, they packaged their beer in one-litre, clear glass bottles with a flip-top, Grolsch-style cap, then in 650-millilitre amber bottles and, since 2006, in 355-millilitre cans. "At first, switching to cans seemed expensive," Patt said. "But Cask Systems of Calgary has developed a canning line that is appropriate for breweries our size. People used to think that cans were only for the big brewers, but they're discovering that cans keep the beer fresher and that they're very eco-friendly. And that fits in with the western Canada outdoor lifestyle. We started canning Anarchist Amber Ale, then the nut brown, and now our IPA."

Cannery brews six year-round beers and three seasonals. A German-style lager, 360, "our hot day beer," as Patt calls it, is brewed with what the website describes as "Mellow Malts and Exciting Hops" and is more robust in flavour than most lagers. It was originally to be called Crystal Creek, to emphasize its clean, crisp finish but when the Dycks found that Molson controlled the rights to that name, they decided on 360, stating,

CanneryBrew

MAPLE
STOUT

NATURALLY BREWED

"It is so crisp that it will change your perspective by 360 degrees."

Cannery's Pale Ale has what Patt refers to as a "lean flavour profile, not too high in IBUs, and with less of a hop bite." An English-style pale ale, it is dark golden in colour and has a noticeable but not too pronounced malty flavour. By contrast, the India Pale Ale, advertised as having "Fierce hops—gentle bite," is noticeably hoppier. Like the pale ale, it is a light- to medium-bodied beer, with refreshing citrus notes. "People were hesitant at first, but we've noted that its popularity is growing as people learn about it and become more adventurous with their beers."

Anarchist Amber Ale, named after a southern Okanagan mountain and described as "disturbingly delicious" is, "a solidly malt beer, featuring a caramel malt. It's not too heavy or too light. People who drink Naramata Nut Brown in the winter often switch to it in the summer." Unlike many amber ales, it has a noticeable hoppy taste, and, as one drinker remarked, "This is what a pale ale would be like if it tried to turn itself into an amber."

Cannery's two other regulars are darker and fuller bodied. Naramata, medium- to full-bodied, has "rich dark malts" with a careful balance of hops to provide a fullness of flavour that is not overwhelming. Blackberry Porter, which began as a seasonal winter warmer and is now the brewery's second-best year-round seller, was likened by one taster to a chocolate-blackberry dessert. It is dark in colour and full-bodied. The flavour of the berries, combined with the three types of hops, prevents it from becoming too heavy. "It's a great after-dinner beer that would go well with dark Belgian chocolate. And you could use it in chocolate cake recipes."

The two seasonal beers are a study in contrasts. Apricot Wheat Beer is designed to soften the citrus flavours noticeable in wheat beers with apricot, making the beer neither overly sweet nor bitter. The wheat lightens the flavour and the hops provide contrast to the malts. Maple Stout, described as "Stout, dark and handsome," is a revival of a traditional British winter ale. Patt offered a poetic description, "Its roasted toastiness has an edge and the addition of maple makes it all sing."

Behind the Tudor exterior of Penticton's Barley Mill Pub are walls covered with amazing collections of historical artifacts from the area as well as sports memorabilia.

The Okanagan's oldest brewpub, **Barley Mill Pub and Sports Bistro** is on a busy thoroughfare that leads into downtown Penticton. The Tudor-style building doesn't look out on spectacular views, but for the sports enthusiast and local history buff, the inside of the building, with its beamed ceilings and wood floors, is a treasure house. Autographed jerseys of such long-ago NHL greats as Guy Lafleur, Rocket Richard, and Jean Béliveau share wall space with old hockey, field hockey, and lacrosse sticks, old photographs of the area, western tack, apple-picking ladders, trophy heads of moose and other big game animals, and, last but certainly not least, historical beer posters. A family-style restaurant occupies the main floor; upstairs is an adults-only pub and the brewing system. There is a pool table, a large stone fireplace and, of course, there are several television screens. At the upstairs and downstairs bars are taps for the five regularly brewed beers and a seasonal beer, and for Coors Lite, Keith's, Heineken, and Guinness. "Some of our regulars, who've been coming here for years, have never tried our own brews," general manager Kevin Hatfield commented.

In 1982, former World Hockey Association player Larry Lund and Harley Hatfield, Kevin's father, began the business as a small neighbourhood pub. Then, in the 1996, the duo decided to transform it into a brewpub. "That way, the seating could be expanded," Kevin Hatfield said. They could also capitalize on the ambience that would be created by having a neighbourhood pub that brewed its own beer. As well, brewing their own was considerably cheaper than purchasing all their beers from megabrewers.

With the help of brewing consultant Mike Tymchuk, founder of Wild Rose Brewery, they developed a line of beers that would offer a departure from the standard fare without being so different as to alienate customers. A mild pale ale, similar to that brewed by Okanagan Spring, a filtered wheat beer that had many lager-like qualities, and a mild English-style brown ale were the first three offerings. Later, they added their first lagers—Caballero Cerveza Lager and Classic Draft Lager.

Ray Huson, the current brewmaster, a homebrewer who left his job as a Penticton area bartender "to get paid to do my hobby," said, "It still amazes me that you start with water and a bunch of stuff in bags and end with so many wonderful things to drink." Summing up his creations, Huson remarked, "You want your beers to be interesting but you can't go too far from the centre if you want [them] to sell. So we straddle the middle, offering a range from our lagers to our brown ale."

The Classic Lager "was designed to be close to the mainstream without the adjuncts the 'big guys' use. We add a little more hops and make it a little darker than mainstream beers." Caballero Cerveza Lager was created to compete with the very popular Mexican import, Corona. "We use a pilsner malt to make it less bland than the Mexican beer, but we make sure it has a very low hop profile. It's a good way to convert our drinkers of mainstream products." Cayuse Wheat Ale is filtered, giving it a clear appearance that appeals to those not used to more traditional cloudy wheat styles.

Barley Mill Pale Ale and Nite Mare Brown Ale are for those drinkers who have already "crossed over." "The pale is our biggest seller. It's moderately hopped. You'd never call it an IPA. But," and he smiled, "if you compared it to a pale ale produced by one of the big brewers, it would seem very hoppy." It is maltier than the in-house beers he'd

Although Ridge Brew House's exterior is Mediterranean-style,
the interior is fairly standard sports bar décor.

already described, but there is a noticeable hop finish. "Our brown ale
is picking up, particularly with climbers and hikers. And it's growing in
popularity in the winter. It started mild, but we've gradually amped it
up, increasing the caramel, chocolate, and black malts. But it isn't over
the top. You could say that it's this side of porter and stout." Huson has
also created three seasonals, using local produce as additives: raspberries,
cherries, and red clover honey.

❖

Osoyoos's Ridge Brew House, located at the intersection of Highways
3 and 97, is easily visible to traffic coming from north, south, east, and
west. Part of a resort complex, it's a Mediterranean-style building, with
a terra cotta tiled roof and white exterior walls that are decorated with
paintings of grape vines. Motel rooms surrounding three sides of the
large parking lot are generally full during the fall and spring when the
complex is the headquarters for popular tours of the area's many golf
courses.

The brewhouse is divided into three sections: a bar and pub, a dining room, and a dining loft. A large gas fireplace takes up nearly all of one wall; behind the floor-to-ceiling panes of glass of another wall stands the ten-hectolitre brewing system. Windows look out on a patio from which the town, Lake Osoyoos, and Anarchist Mountain are visible. Television sets, most turned to sports channels, are strategically placed throughout the building. A pool table and dart boards offer standard pub entertainment.

Owner-manager Ken Lormer observed that the establishment serves two distinct groups. "For the locals, this is a place to come to eat. And, because people here are very loyal Budweiser and Kokanee drinkers, we have taps for those beers. But, because Osoyoos is also a holiday destination, we want to give our visitors a taste of the Lower Okanagan. We use local honey and malts from Gambrinus Malting Company north of Vernon. In the summer we've even made beers using lavender flowers from the area, and seasonal fruits. We don't want our beers to be extreme."

Brewer Shirley Warne, who flies in from Vancouver when it's time to start a new brew, noted that the three best-selling beers follow style guidelines closely. Moreover, because of the hard water, with its high magnesium and iron content, it is difficult to create the more highly hopped beers she prefers. "I think that most of the customers are older drinkers who have fixed tastes. If they don't drink 'commercial' beers, they want something that is a crossover, not too different from familiar tastes."

Ridge Genuine Draft, RGD "is a very low-hopped beer," Warne commented. Light-bodied and light gold in colour, it is very close in taste and mouth-feel to the lagers produced by mainstream brewers. Honey Ale has a noticeable honey aftertaste. Amberdillo, a medium-bodied amber, is similar to a pale ale, while the India Pale Ale is much less hopped than most examples of the style. 'O' Town Brown has hints of chocolate and coffee. None of the beers is assertive, instead seeking to gently introduce microbrewed styles to those unfamiliar with them.

Okanagan Spring Brewery
    2808 27th Ave, Vernon, V1T 9K4, 250-542-2337, okspring,com
Tree Brewing Company
    1083 Richter St, Kelowna, V1Y 2K6, 800-663-4847, treebeer.com

Granville Island Brewing Company
   1125 Richter St, Kelowna, V1Y 2K6, 250-762-3332, gib.ca
Freddy's Brewpub/Mill Creek Brewery
   124 – 948 McCurdy Rd, Kelowna, V1X 2P7, 250-765-8956, mccurdybowl.com
Tin Whistle Brewing Company
   954 Eckhardt Ave, Penticton, V2A 2C1, 250-770-1122
Cannery Brewing Company
   112 – 1475 Fairview Rd, Penticton, V2A 7W5, 250-473-2723, cannerybrewing.com
Barley Mill Pub and Sports Bistro
   2460 Skaha Lake Rd, Penticton, V2A 6E8, 250-493-8000, barleymillpub.com
Ridge Brew House
   9913 Highway 3, Osoyoos, V0H 1V0, 800-977-8711, westridgeinn.com

CHAPTER FIVE

Trans-Canada Ales
Revelstoke to Kamloops; Prince George to Smithers
(with a Visit to Whitehorse)

In the mid-1990s, Tracey and Bart Larson left the crowded and stressful environment of Greater Vancouver and retreated to Bart's hometown of Revelstoke to start a microbrewery. After earning a doctorate in nuclear physics, Bart had discovered few post-doctorate opportunities in his field in Canada and turned to his love of making beer. For Tracey, who has a Bachelor of Science degree, the move gave her a chance enjoy her hobbies of hiking and mountain biking. They opened **Mt. Begbie Brewing Company** in 1996, almost four decades after Enterprise Brewery, the town's last brewing company, had closed. When the Larsons began their business, Revelstoke was still a small town, although it was beginning to become a year-round tourist destination. "We were fairly isolated when we opened," Tracey remembered. "We had to ship everything in and, even though we quickly developed a loyal following from local businesses, we had to transport our beer to other places." Competition was tough: in the Okanagan, Tree and Tin Whistle had recently begun operations; Bear had opened a year earlier in Kamloops.

The first year, Mt. Begbie operated with a staff of one and a half: Brad brewed and delivered kegs in the area; Tracey spent half of her time running the brewery office and the other half working as a veterinary assistant, "so we could put food on the table." First-year production was five hundred hectolitres, nearly all of it Begbie Cream Ale. "We wanted to start with something lager-like, but with more depth," Bart explained. "The local market wasn't ready for the more extreme beers that were popular in Victoria and Vancouver. At first, the cream ale was quite hoppy, but we had to tone it down." A light-bodied, golden ale, smooth and not too malty, it served as what Brad referred to as a "stepping stone" for drinkers of mainstream beers. The use of honey malts gives a slightly sweet flavour and wheat malt contributes to the smooth finish.

"The Falcons" hockey team, Revels

**Brewed right here in the spectacular Co
this pale German-style Kölschbier is a r
quencher. No preservatives or addit**

4.5% alc./vol. beer

Tracey Larson jokingly reminds husband Bart that, in a brewery,
"cleanliness is next to godliness" and pretends to hose him down.
The couple founded Revelstoke's Mt. Begbie Brewing in 1996.

The Larsons realized that they needed something to appeal to
drinkers of Kokanee. They decided on Kolsch, a relatively little-known
German style that Bart had discovered when he was taking a brewing
course at Chicago's Siebel Institute. A clear, crisp, light-bodied ale, it

resembles a lager. However, the 20 per cent wheat malt and subtle use of hops give it ale characteristics. "This is what a lager would be like if it decided to become an ale," laughed one taster. High Country Kolsch quickly became a bestseller. When the Larsons, who had introduced 650-millilitre bottles after two years of production, decided in 2009 to can their products, High Country Kolsch was the first to be packaged in the new containers.

Mt. Begbie's two other year-round beers move beyond crossovers. Powerhouse Pale Ale began its life as Alpine Pale Ale, until Moosehead Breweries informed the Larsons that, even though Revelstoke was known as the Alpine City, the East Coast brewery owned the rights to that name, which it applied to a value-priced brand. Powerhouse is less hoppy than similar brews that come from the West Coast. "We try not to be stupidly hoppy," Bart noted. "We want a balance of hops and malts—that's something our market appreciates more." Tall Timber Ale, an English brown, is, at 5.2 per cent ABV, the strongest of the brewery's regular offerings. "At first, we kept the carbonation low like the English do, but people thought it was flat so we increased it to North American standards. We use six or seven malts, giving it a complex flavour profile, and just enough hops to balance out the sweetness of the malts."

Speaking of his limited use of hops, Bart said, "We are driven by our market. I like hops, but we have to look at sales. What's important for us is drinkability; when you've finished one of our beers, the taste should make you want another. It's the flavour, not the alcohol, that you appreciate. Our core beers offer good, solid traditional tastes. In our seasonals, we have fun; we can experiment and vary those from year to year. In 2009, we put out an IPA that we called 'Nasty Habit.' It was different."

❖

Drivers coming into Salmon Arm from the west can't miss Barley Station Brew Pub. Designed to look like an old-time railroad station with hop vines climbing up one of the walls, it stands next to the Trans-Canada Highway at the edge of downtown. Patrons looking out of the spacious windows or sitting on the summer patio can see not only the highway traffic rolling by, but also Shuswap Lake and the nearby mountains.

"When we moved to Salmon Arm in 1998, we thought about

Brewmaster Don Moore enjoys one of his creations as he stands next to the hop vines that adorn one of the walls at Salmon Arm's Barley Station Brew Pub.

a brewpub," remarked Stu Bradford, co-owner, with his wife, Kathy, of Barley Station. "The building had been a restaurant, and, when it became vacant a few years ago, we decided to buy it. Salmon Arm was ready for something different. It was becoming a tourist destination, and thousands of people travelling from the coast to Alberta passed the building every day. The town was becoming home to more and more retirees, people we felt would be attracted to a brewpub." The brewing arm of the establishment was named Shuswap Lake Brewing.

Don Moore, the person they hired as brewmaster, had nearly a quarter-of-century's experience as a professional brewer under his belt, especially with small, new microbreweries and brewpubs, most recently Fernie and Jasper Brewing. "I like new, creative, small breweries," he remarked. He emphasized that he followed traditional styles, "as I interpret them." Initially, he developed four pale beers: a pilsner, a blonde, a pale ale, and a *wit*, styles that would serve as good introductions to unfamiliar types of beer. According to information on the restaurant's placemat, Station House Blonde "emulates the lagers of the larger breweries of North America." Light-bodied and pale yellow, it provides consumers of mainstream beers an entry into microbrews. Canoe Creek Pilsner, named after a small stream on the Bradfords' farm, is a complex lager. A German pilsner with a crisp hop finish, it is brewed with all organic ingredients, including malts from Gambrinus Malting in nearby Armstrong. Talking Dog Wit, named after one of the Bradfords' pets, is a Belgian-style ale, in which notes of coriander dominate. Popular in the summer, it is cloudy in appearance.

Shuswap Lake's other two year-round brews move away from the light and fairly familiar. Bushwacker Brown Ale, an English brown, blends eight malts to create a chocolatey, nutty flavour. Sam McGuire's Pale Ale, named after a local pioneer, is described as "a big bodied beer with huge hops throughout." Moore noted that the use of five different hops, each added at a different stage of the brewing process, created fruity, flowery aromas.

❖

Left Fields Farm, east of Kamloops near the village of Sorrento, is the home of **Crannog Ales**, Canada's first certified organic brewery. Named after the elevated huts constructed above Irish bogs, the brewery employs three people, including co-owners Rebecca Kneen and Brian MacIsaac, produces just over 800 hectolitres a year, and deliberately avoids packaging its products in bottles and cans. "We think drinking beer is a social event," said MacIsaac, who calls himself an ale smith to distinguish himself from a brewmaster, who would have received a diploma from a certified institution. "We'd like people to enjoy each other's company with our beer. We don't like the idea of someone buying a six-pack and going home to drink alone."

Although small, Left Fields is a working farm from which come some of the ingredients used in brewing. In fact, it was Kneen's desire to return to the land that led to the formation of the brewery. She'd been working with FarmFolkCityFolk, a non-profit organization in the Vancouver area that seeks to reduce the distance from source to plate of the food people eat. "To create the kind of small, self-sustaining organic farm I wanted would require some kind of off-farm source of income. That's where Brian came in."

Brian MacIsaac, who'd played in rock bands, studied art after high

The raised building in the foreground is a crannog, a traditional Irish structure built over a bog. The brewery building in the background is decorated with Celtic designs created by Brian MacIsaac, co-founder of Crannog Ales.

school and been a social worker, had homebrewed for a dozen years before turning professional. He worked on a volunteer basis at Vancouver's Storm Brewing in order to learn about larger-scale professional brewing and then trained at the American Brewers Guild in Sacramento, California.

The two partners first developed a philosophy and then a business plan to integrate farming and brewing. Sorrento was chosen, Kneen said, "because it reminded me of my childhood home in the Maritimes, and there was a strong, supportive organic agricultural community in the area." Left Fields Farm had a building just the right size to house a small brewery—they thought. "But the law said it exceeded the square footage allowed for an on-farm business, so we lopped ten feet off one end." Then they met with liquor officials. "We were at one meeting with members of three different branches of the liquor board, and they started arguing with each other." They purchased used equipment from Horseshoe Bay Brewery, Canada's first brewpub, and hired pioneering microbrewer John Mitchell to help them set it up.

Two principles were paramount in the establishment and then in the running of both Left Fields Farm and Crannog Ales: the two together should be as self-sustaining as possible and both should be completely organic. The pigs, for example, would eat the spent grains from the brewing process; their waste would be used, where feasible, for fertilizer; and they would provide food. The farm would produce the hops for the brewing process and grow the various fruits and vegetables used by the family, and the bees they raised would produce honey used in some of the beers. Water from the on-farm well would be used in the brewery, treated, and then reused. The sustainability program is exemplified by the annual "One Hundred Foot Table" dinner Crannog holds each August. The one hundred feet refer to the distance that most of the food and beverages have to travel from their source to the table.

"I think that both the farm and the brewery are a celebration and exploration of the land," Kneen remarked. "There's also a political aspect. When people learn about our brewery or visit the farm, they see examples of how to form a partnership with the land." The brewery opened in 2000, the year after it received its organic certification from the Pacific Agricultural Certification Society. Crannog's status must be reaffirmed through twice-yearly inspections.

Crannog's ales are what MacIsaac calls "a sharing of my Celtic-Gaelic heritage." Although born in Burnaby, he spent several of his childhood years in Belfast. As a young adult visiting Expo 67 in Montreal, he discovered Guinness and later he learned about other, lesser-known Irish beers that weren't readily available in Canada. He used Red Branch Irish Ale as an example of what he set out to introduce to Canadian beer drinkers. "We wanted to go to an Irish style from the sixteenth century. North American versions of the style use food colouring and caramel malts and most are over-hopped." He also sought to avoid rigid consistency from brew to brew. "Variables are important in beer just as in wine. We want people to celebrate differences; we don't want to McDonaldize our styles." Just as ingredients may vary from crop to crop, so do the beers brewed from them. "We just picked a batch of hops a week ago and they'll help to create a different taste than if we'd used some that had been stored for a while."

Crannog's Irish focus is initially evident to visitors to the farm in the ornate, stylized Celtic designs MacIsaac has created to adorn the farm buildings and in a brochure describing the ales and the names given to them, names such as Hell's Kitchen (an Irish district in nineteenth-century New York), Red Branch (after legendary Irish heroes), and Back

Hand of God (a Gaelic expression indicating great surprise). Some of the names created controversy. A few Vancouver bars objected to the name Hell's Kitchen, noting that a well-known local restaurant had the same name and they didn't want to give it free advertising. The Liquor Control Board at first felt that the term Back Hand of God was sacrilegious.

The essential Irish aspect of Crannog is in the beers themselves, which recreate centuries-old styles. Red Branch, one of the brewery's first two products, is an Irish red ale. "It's our mildest ale," MacIsaac noted. "We wanted to give it a slight burnt-sugar taste and to introduce caramel malts with a hint of sugar." Beyond the Pale Ale began as a bitter, but when people objected to the high hop content, Brian modified it. "We used our own hops to make a fresher, lighter ale. It has low carbonation and is easy drinking." Ironically, although the term "beyond the Pale" refers to areas outside where the English settled in Northern Ireland (in other words, the homes of the "wild" Irish), the recipe is based on one brought to Ireland by Yorkshire immigrants.

Bog Trotter Brown Ale is Crannog's way of helping people explore the variety of malt tastes in a beer and emphasizes chocolate and dark caramel malts. Lightly hopped and, at 4.9 per cent ABV, low in alcohol content, it is designed as a session beer. By contrast, Hell's Kitchen at 5.2 per cent ABV is much heartier. It contains that traditional Irish dietary staple, potatoes. "We briefly cook up unpeeled russet potatoes and then put them in the mash to finish the cooking. That releases starches into the brew. The potatoes also give an earthy taste to the beer."

Surprisingly, Back Hand of God Stout is Crannog's most popular brew, accounting for half of its sales. "People doubted that we could make a go of a stout in the interior of BC. We worked to make it not like Guinness. It's not created from a sour mash, so it isn't bitter. In fact, it has hints of sweetness and some coffee and chocolate notes. It's less carbonated and less hopped than other stouts, and it has a smoothness that makes it very drinkable."

MacIsaac says of Crannog ales that they are for initiated, sophisticated drinkers who are looking for flavour. "We want our beers to be paired with complementary meals. That way, they become part of the social aspect of the dining experience." But if you want to enjoy both the Irish experience and the social interaction that are part of drinking

Northam Brewery, in Kamloops, brews Whistler, Bowen Island, and Kamloops beers. The small white tank to the left of two larger ones contains water that is shipped from the town of Whistler for the brewing of the Whistler brands.

Crannog's ales, you can't just stop at your local liquor store for a six-pack. You'll have to visit one of the growing number of bars that carry the line or drop by Left Fields Farm, become part of the community of their One Hundred Foot Table, and later pick up a party pig to share with friends.

The landscape around the brewery perched on a hillside in an industrial park in southwestern Kamloops looks like neither Whistler, the famous ski resort town, nor Bowen Island, in Howe Sound. However, a sign identifies the structure as **Northam Brewery,** the main production centre for Whistler and Bowen Island beers.

In 1995, David Beardsell opened Bear Brewing, the first brewery in Kamloops since Imperial Brewery closed in 1927. Beardsell created English-style beers, each one named after the colour of a bear—black, brown, golden, and polar—to indicate not only the beer's colour, but also its style. Meanwhile, Whistler Brewing, which had been founded in 1989, and Bowen Island Brewing Company, which had started business in 1994, merged, and consolidated their brewing operations in Whistler in 1999.

In the spring of 2001, the picture became more complicated. Calgary's Big Rock Brewery, seeking to strengthen its business in BC, purchased Whistler Brewing and announced that it had signed a licensing agreement with Bear Brewing to brew the Whistler and Bowen Island products at the Kamloops plant. A year later, it purchased Bear Brewing. However, in 2005, after anticipated changes in BC's liquor laws did not materialize and Big Rock's hopes of brewing its own brands in Kamloops disappeared, it sold its Bear, Whistler, and Bowen Island properties to Northam.

The Whistler and Bowen Island brands grew in popularity, but three of the Bear brands became extinct. Now only Black Bear, a dark ale infused with blackberries, is easily available. Meanwhile, Northam opened a new, smaller plant in Whistler in time to capitalize on the 2010 Winter Olympics. The bulk of production still takes place at the Kamloops brewery, with water brought in tanks from Whistler in order to make the brand more than just a name. (Discussion of the beers brewed under the Whistler label can be found on pages 168–172.)

Bowen Island has become Northam's value-priced product. Distributed in cans and priced considerably lower than the Whistler brands, it is designed to compete with Labatt's extremely popular Lucky Lager. Five styles are brewed. Bowen Island Lager is a light-bodied, highly carbonated, fairly standard North American pale lager. Extra Pale Ale, an English-style beer, is light- to medium-bodied and dark amber in colour. Irish Cream Ale is a medium brown ale that has stronger malt notes than the first two and a noticeable hop finish. Honey Brown Lager, an American dark lager, has strong malt flavours and more than a taste of honey. Special Light is a fairly standard light lager.

❖

In 1955, Prince George's first brewery, Nechako Brewery, the predecessor of what is now Pacific Western Brewing, opened. A year later, it became Caribou Brewing, and in 1961, it was purchased and then closed by Carling-O'Keefe. Ben Ginter bought the building to house his company's construction equipment, but soon decided to resurrect the brewery, which he named Tartan. In 1978, financial difficulties forced him to shut it down. Subsequent owners called it Prince George Brewing, Gold Crown, and Old Fort Brewing. It became Pacific Western Brewing in 1984. Purchased in 1986 by Potter Distilling, it was sold in 1991 to Pacific Pinnacle Investments, a firm owned by Japanese-Canadian Kazuko Komatsu, which exported BC products to Asian markets. Under her leadership, the company grew, expanding foreign markets to 40 per cent of its production by the mid-1990s. The rising Canadian dollar has since caused a decrease in exports.

With the exception of Natureland Amber Ale and Natureland Lager, both organic beers, and Pacific Dry, a Japanese-style lager, Pacific Western's main beers are fairly standard lagers, designed to appeal to provincial drinkers who prefer lagers to ales by a nine to one ratio. The company's most recent beer, Cariboo Genuine Draft, highlights this focus. "We wanted to create a beer that British Columbians could call our own. One that reflected our rugged terrain, majestic scenery, and the working spirit of the people in the province." Three of the lagers are strong beers: TNT (available in both 8 per cent ABV and 6 per cent versions) and Iron Horse (6.4 per cent ABV). One of Pacific Western's brews fits into the niche category: Canterbury Dark Mild is a European dark lager.

❖

Plan B Brewing in Smithers is almost the complete opposite of Pacific Western with its fifty employees, hundred thousand-hectolitre annual production, and almost complete focus on varieties of lagers. Mark Gillis and Glen Ingram, Plan B's two employees, who are also the co-owners, brew just three hundred litres a week of four beers, all of which are ales. "We are a small, part-time brewery that serves our local community," Ingram explained.

Ingram, a Smithers native, began homebrewing with the help of a local brew-on-premises business, discovered the wonderful variety of beer styles while studying in Victoria and Minneapolis, and decided that he would try to duplicate in his homebrews the qualities of those beers he liked best. A computer program developer, he returned to Smithers, met Mark Gillis, and the two began developing recipes and brewing in Gillis's garage. "He liked the darker ales; I liked paler ones.

Glen Ingram (above) and Mark Gillis opened Plan B Brewing in Smithers
to offer area residents alternatives to the pale North American lagers
that were most readily available in northern British Columbia.

PHOTO COURTESY OF GLEN INGRAM

So we complemented each other." When their operations became too
large for the garage, they looked for a place to rent and decided to brew
commercially on a part-time basis, using the revenue to pay for renting
a place and the costs of supplies and larger equipment.

In the fall of 2009, Plan B was born, the name perhaps a play on the term for the morning-after contraceptive pill, with the "B," of course, referring to beer. The main idea was, as Ingram put it, "that people can have a plan B and not know it. That's us and the brewery." Open only three days and a total of fourteen hours a week, Plan B was designed to offer the local community—which Ingram described as being much more diverse in backgrounds and interests than most of the places along Highway 16—alternatives to the mass-produced lagers found in bars and liquor stories. Available only from the brewery, the beers are sold in kegs and one-litre Grolsch-style bottles.

The four ales Plan B creates reflect the different preferences of the two brewers. Revenge of the Pine Pale Ale (named as a salute to the trees that struggled against the ravages of the mountian pine beetle) and Idiot Rock IPA (a reference to a favourite local fishing spot) are Ingram's inspirations. "We wanted to start off with a good pale as our base—something that people could enjoy on a daily basis." It's a cross between American and Canadian West Coast ales, more hopped than Canadian versions and less carbonated than such well-known American examples as Sierra Nevada and Bridgeport. It is also darker than most pale ales, almost amber in colour. The IPA is strongly hopped; the Centennial hops used in the dry-hopping give it a citrusy aroma and taste.

The name for Half Cracked Nut Brown Ale, Gillis's creation, comes from a song enjoyed by his children, which contains the line "I'm a nut, half-cracked." "That's us, starting a brewery," Ingram laughed. "The label has a picture of the two of us wearing our aprons, with Napoleon-type hats on our heads." He described the beer as being half-way between their pale ale and stout. "It's very much an English-style brown, with low carbonation. We use hops, but subtly, and there's very little bitterness." McHugh's Oatmeal Stout is a tribute to Gillis's wife, who agreed to take his name after they were married if he named a beer after her. "This beer has become a favourite in the community. They find it much easier to drink than they expected. It has a creamy mouth-feel, and chocolate and coffee notes. It's a nice balance between bitter and sweet."

During the twentieth century, countless thousands of pints of beer were downed in the Land of the Midnight Sun. But between 1916, when O'Brien's Brewing and Malting of Dawson City closed, and 1997, when what is now called **Yukon Brewing Company** opened, all of those pints that had been brewed legally came from outside Yukon Territory. The idea for a new brewery in the territory that had the highest per capita beer consumption of any province or territory in Canada came to Bob Baxter and Alan Hansen, two homebrewing friends, while on a canoe trip in the southern Yukon. They would create quality beers, build a customer base centred in Whitehorse, and export product to neighbouring provinces, Alaska, and the Northwest Territories. It would be relatively easy to bring in malt, hops, and yeast; the area had great water; and the cost for shipping beer out would not be overwhelming if they used empty trucks returning to BC and Alberta after they had delivered their freight to Whitehorse.

In 1997, the two opened Chilkoot Brewing, offering a honey pale and an amber ale. "We had to be gentle at first," Baxter remembered. "People weren't quite ready for fuller-flavoured, different-tasting beers. Then, after we'd been around a couple of years, local people asked us to make a lager, a plain old beer. So we made a European lager. It was a beautifully round, full beer but people didn't take to it, and we had to dumb it down, to make it more mainstream. Now, they're ready for something different—for something full of flavour. In the Yukon, people are very supportive of local businesses, as long as the goods or services you offer are top quality. We sell more draft beer in the Yukon than Molson and Labatt combined."

As the brewery grew—it now produces over six thousand five hundred hectolitres a year and employs fifteen people—it underwent two name changes. The Chilkoot name was replaced by Cheechako. "The first was too regional, but for the second, you really had to have been in the Yukon or Alaska to know what it referred to, and nobody could spell Cheechako," Baxter laughed. In 1999, it became Yukon. That name was recognized far beyond territorial borders and carried with it connotations of spectacular scenery and outdoor adventure. Sales grew, both in the Yukon and "Outside."

Yukon Brewing produces seven regular beers, each of which, according to the company slogan is a "beer worth freezin' for." Baxter was more specific in describing the overall characteristics of the brews. "Our beers are very dry, not sweet; we like a sharp, crisp flavour. Each one is a distinctive example of its style."

Yukon Red, the brewery's best seller outside the Yukon, was named the Canadian Beer of the Year in 2009. It's a medium-bodied, amber to red Irish-style ale, with a balance between the malts, with their chocolate and coffee notes, and the hops. Yukon Gold, the best seller in the Yukon, is an English-style pale ale. Dark gold to amber in colour, it has rich malt flavours with a crisp hop finish that is not too bitter. "If you want to know what the big guys would produce if they left the additives [adjuncts] out, give Chilkoot a try," says the website about Yukon's competition against the beers sold by Molson and Labatt. Chilkoot Lager has some malt sweetness, but is low on both flavour and hop bitterness.

Lead Dog Ale and Midnight Sun Espresso Stout move into the darker-coloured areas. The former is a 7 per cent ABV English winter ale that uses six different malts. The latter uses eight malts and oatmeal, along with espresso coffee ground locally. It is one of four of the brewery's beers that use Yukon products. In fact, it was Midnight Sun Coffee Roasters that suggested the additive for the beer. Discovery Ale, the company's first beer, is a honey pale ale that uses Yukon fireweed honey. Cranberry Wheat Ale is flavoured by Yukon cranberries when they are available; the berries give a dry tartness not unlike that of some Belgian ales. "Cranberries in a beer?" the website copy asks. "Why not—all those Yukon bears can't be wrong." Perhaps the most unusual of Yukon's locally flavoured beers is their late spring Birch Beer. "One of our customers, who tapped birch trees each spring, came to us with the idea. It's like a maple-flavoured beer, but much more tart. Every spring people ask us when it's coming out. When it does, it isn't around for long," Baxter noted.

Mt. Begbie Brewing Company
   521 West 1st St, Revelstoke, V0E 2S0, 250-837-2756, mt-begbie.com
Barley Station Brew Pub/Shuswap Lake Brewing
   20 Shuswap St SE, Salmon Arm, V1E 4H7, 250-832-0999, barleystation.com
Crannog Ales
   706 Elson Rd, Sorrento, V0E 2W0, 250-675-6847, crannogales.com

Northam Brewery
    McGill Pl, Kamloops, V2C 6N9, 250-851-2543
Pacific Western Brewing
    641 N Nechako Rd, Prince George, V2K 4M4, 250-562-2424, pwbrewing.net
Plan B Brewing
    3352 Highway 16, Smithers, V0J 2N0, 250-877-7873, planbbrewing.com
Yukon Brewing Company
    102A Copper Rd, Whitehorse, YT, Y1A 2Z6, 867-668-4183, yukonbeer.com

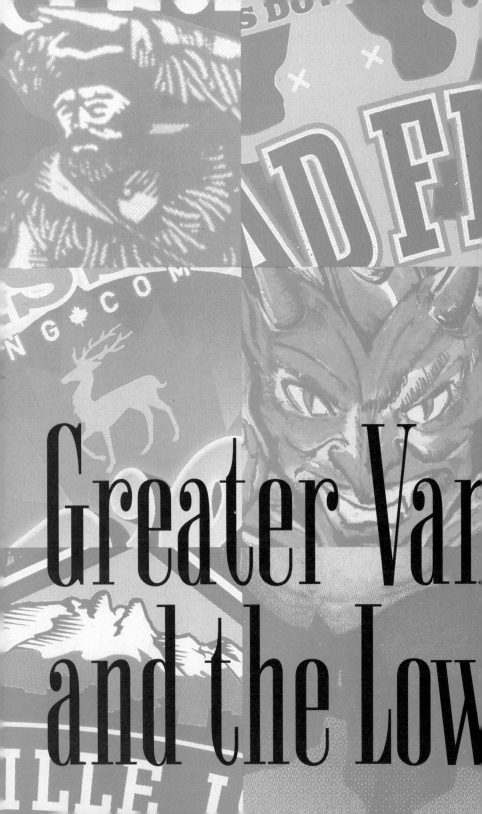

Greater Van
and the Low

ORIGINAL

K TUSK

BR

couver
er Mainland

(BREWING

Part Three

Greater Vancouver and the Lower Mainland

In 1860, two years after Victoria Brewery had become the first brewery west of what is now Ontario, the Lower Mainland's first brewery opened in New Westminster. Vancouver's first brewery opened in 1887.

Two of the Lower Mainland's nineteenth-century breweries had very long histories. In 1897, Nels Nelson purchased a New Westminster brewery that had begun operations in 1879 as Sapperton Brewery. He renamed it Westminster Brewery and it operated at the same location throughout the twentieth century. In 1930, it was sold to the Coast Brewery group, which renamed the operation Lucky Lager Brewery in 1950. In 1958, Labatt purchased the brewery as part of its westward expansion and ran it until 2005, when it was closed down.

City Brewery of Vancouver, founded in 1887 and renamed Red Cross Brewery a few years later, merged in 1900 with Vancouver Brewery, which had been founded in 1889 by Charles Doering and Otto Marstrand. It operated under the name Vancouver Breweries for a decade before becoming part of a newly formed consortium: British Columbia Breweries. It remained in business under a variety of names and owners until 1957, when it was purchased by Carling Breweries, which was also expanding westward. The plant closed in 1990 when Carling-O'Keefe merged with Molson.

In 1934, Fritz and Emil Sick, who had founded breweries in Alberta, Saskatchewan, and eastern British Columbia, began operating Capilano Brewery in Vancouver. In 1953, production was moved a new plant near the southwest end of the Burrard Street Bridge. In 1958, the brewery was sold to Molson, which had also acquired Sick breweries in Edmonton and Lethbridge.

In 1982, with the founding of Horseshoe Bay Brewery and Troller Pub by John Mitchell and his partners, a new era of BC brewing history began. While the three national brewers still controlled well over 90 per cent of the market, consumers were now able to enjoy domestically produced beers that weren't pale North American lagers. From 1982 to the summer of 2010, a total of thirty microbreweries and brewpubs opened in twelve cities and villages from Whistler to Chilliwack. In the summer of 2010, ten brewpubs, two of which operated microbreweries, and eight microbreweries were in operation. Molson, now part of an international brewing corporation, along with its American partners, Miller and Coors, is the only megabrewery on the Lower Mainland.

CHAPTER SIX

Ale-ong the Fraser River
Chilliwack to Richmond

Goose Bay, Labrador, and Chico, California, may seem like unusual towns to call the birthplaces of Chilliwack's **Old Yale Brewing Company**. However, during the 1980s, when Larry Caza, the company's owner, brewmaster, and one of its three employees, was stationed at the Canadian Armed Forces base on Canada's east coast, he discovered a whole new world of beer. "Some of us used to drink with the European pilots who train there. One of them had brought over some bottles of Budvar from Czechoslovakia. I didn't know what it was, but it certainly had flavour."

He quickly lost his taste for the North American lagers he'd been drinking and decided that upon his return to his hometown of Chilliwack he'd begin homebrewing. Not long afterwards, on a driving trip through California, he discovered Sierra Nevada Pale Ale, one of the pioneer beers of the American microbrewing movement. "I was sitting in the passenger seat drinking a bottle, really enjoying its hoppy flavour, when I noticed that it was brewed in Chico and that we were driving close to there. My friend and I stopped at their brewpub and were amazed at the wonderful beers they made. I thought to myself, 'We need a microbrewery in Chilliwack.'"

In 2000, he opened Old Yale Brewing Company in one hundred and thirty square metres of space in a small building south of Chilliwack. Named after a historic wagon road that stretched from Vancouver to Yale, the brewery began as a local operation, producing draft beer for Chilliwack and nearby towns. "We named our first product Chilliwack Blonde Ale, because we wanted to emphasize that we were local, that we were different from the national brands."

Although the brewery's products are now available throughout BC in 650-millilitre bottles, their names reflect local geography, history, and folklore: Sergeant's IPA pays tribute to the military base that used to be kitty-corner to where the brewery is located; Sasquatch Stout to the mythical creature said to inhabit the area's forests and mountains; and Cultus Lake Pilsner to a popular nearby recreation area.

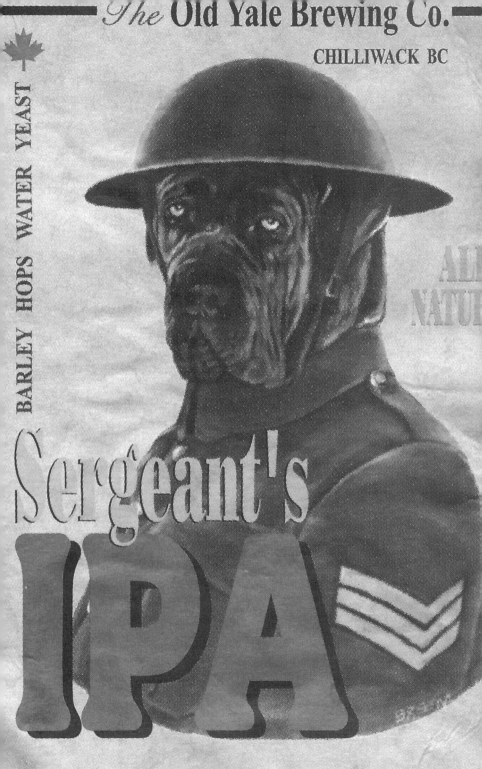

Although Old Yale Brewing produces only seven hundred and fifty hectolitres a year, it has earned five Canadian Brewing Awards gold medals, one of which owner Larry Caza is wearing around his neck.

Much as Caza would have liked to brew one, Old Yale's first beer wasn't a Sierra Nevada-inspired pale ale. "Chilliwack wasn't ready for hops then. In a way, we had to sneak gently into town with a beer that was light-bodied, refreshing, and smooth. We needed something that would gradually introduce local beer drinkers to microbrews." Chilliwack Blonde was phased out after a few years and replaced in 2006 by Cultus Lake Pilsner.

Caza developed and introduced two variations of his favourite style, pale ale. "I modelled Old Yale Pale Ale on Sierra Nevada. There was nothing like it being brewed in the Lower Mainland. It was hoppy, but not overwhelming." An amber-coloured, light- to medium-bodied ale, with a balance between hops and malts, it is crisp finishing. Sergeant's IPA, at 5.5 per cent ABV, is a little stronger than the pale ale, has a photograph of Caza's dog dressed in a Second World War army uniform on the label, and has "loads of Golding hops inside the bottle." A gold-coloured ale with a noticeable hop finish, it is smooth and mellow.

Sasquatch Stout was designed to round out Old Yale's portfolio of ales. "We had the pale and the IPA and wanted a darker, more full-bodied beer. People think Guinness is thick—ours is thicker. Somebody told us that it reminded them of a chocolate milkshake. The chocolate, coffee, and roasty flavours all come from the malts, and the oatmeal gives it its creaminess. I've been really pleased and surprised with the response from young people and from people who don't usually drink beer. They love it." The bottle description notes that it is black and robust "with a lot of body, just like the mysterious animal itself."

Cultus Lake Pilsner was created because "we had three ales and needed a crisper, lighter beer. It's our white wine to our red wine ales— something that a Bud drinker would be comfortable with." Caza noted that it's at the bottom end of the pilsner category, without the subtle balancing of hops and malts that characterizes Czech varieties of the style. "But it definitely isn't mainstream."

Old Yale's annual production is around seven hundred and fifty hectolitres. However, being small hasn't prevented the brewery from garnering national and international recognition. Sergeant's IPA won Canadian Brewing Awards gold medals three years in a row; the pale ale and Sasquatch stout have also earned CBA golds. Asked why small breweries consistently win major awards, Caza replied, "Because we do smaller batches than the big brewers, we can tinker with the recipes, offering subtle variations of each style. For us, brewing is 50 per cent science and 50 per cent art."

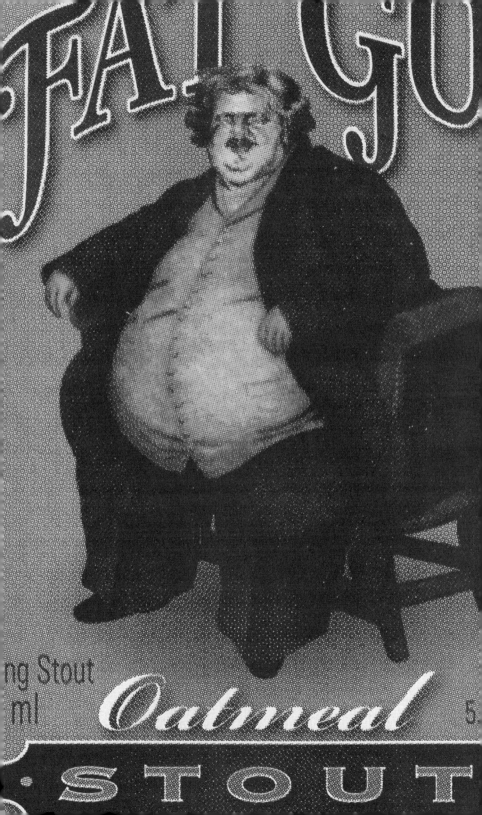

Mission Springs Brewing offers more than good beer and food. For active patrons, there is a beach volleyball court and a three-on-three basketball court. For the inactive, there are a dozen televisions to watch and interesting vintage artifacts to look at.

Thirty kilometres downstream from Chilliwack and across the Fraser River stands **Mission Springs Brewing Company**, along with a restaurant, brewpub, and liquor store. Founded in 1986, it became the Fraser Valley's first brewpub ten years later.

People enjoy the sports activities and historic decor of Mission Springs but they come for the food—good, reasonably priced, substantial pub fare—and the beer created by brewmaster Tim Brown. In the mid-1990s, Brown was the winner of a Mr. Shaftebury look-alike contest put on by the microbrewery of the same name and worked in many promotional appearances it sponsored. "But I became tired of just being an anthropomorphized tap handle," he said. "So I applied for a job as a bartender here at Mission Springs and snuck in to work in the brewery on my off-days." He became the head brewer in 1999.

Mission Springs offers five year-round beers, each one identified by a catchy nickname and visual identification. Big Chief Cream Ale is named after a long-ago service station on Route 66, the historic American highway, and the label of the bottled version of the product (available at the liquor store next door) depicts a Plains Indian wearing a chief's headdress—an image that was found on the signs at the service station. "The beer was designed as an entry level or gateway beer," Brown said. "It has some colour, but a very mild flavour." The label of Bombshell Blonde uses Second World War-style pop art to depict a curvaceous blonde with Betty Grable legs perched atop a fighter plane. Brown proudly announced that the ale has always been the brewpub's best seller. "It's drinkable for everyone." Pale straw in colour, it is light-bodied, effervescent, and crisp. Neither hops nor malts dominate, although there's a sweet malty aftertaste.

Old Sailor IPA, Mission Springs' second-best seller, is a golden, full-flavoured, citrusy drink, with a definite, but not overwhelming, use of hops. Its IBU level is just over fifty. At 5.6 per cent ABV, it is the strongest of the beers. Fat Guy Stout is a creamy oatmeal stout with a complex variety of flavours. Appropriate to the name, the label depicts a very large man dressed in early nineteenth-century English attire. He is barely able fit into his chair, and his wig clings tenuously to the top of his head. The fifth ale, Brewer's Black and Tan, shows a medieval monk tending an open brew kettle. It is a mixture of the pale ale and stout and, because it is mixed after the brewing of the two ales is complete, it has layers of black and copper colours.

❖

Located in Aldergrove, some fifty kilometres west of Old Yale, **Dead Frog Brewery**, unlike Old Yale, wasn't content to stay small. Metaphorically speaking, it could be said that in 2006, a dead frog hopped out of the backwoods to give new life to a brewery whose beer sales had gone flat. Derrick Smith, a homebrewer who'd started Copper Kettle, a brew-on-premises establishment in 1998, formed Backwoods Brewery, a draft-only company selling to pubs and restaurants in the Fraser Valley, soon afterwards.

"People really liked our beer," Smith said, "but after a few years, sales had levelled out." The problem was brand recognition. "Nobody could remember our name—Backwoods, Backwater, Blackwoods, Backwards. And," he chuckled, "we needed something eye-catching, something easy to remember." The company contacted Vancouver's Creative Branding and Design, asking the firm either to redesign Backwoods' image or to

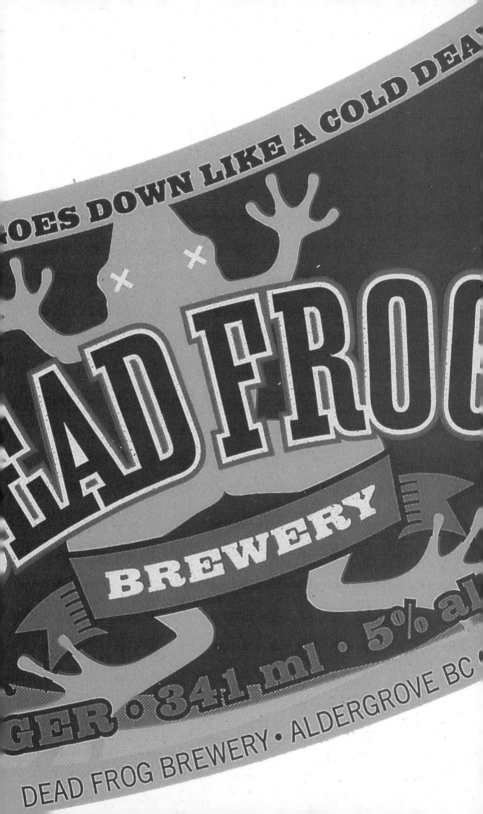

A clever name and catchy slogans have helped make
Dead Frog Brewing one of BC's fastest-growing breweries.

come up with a new name. When Smith and his partners were presented with Creative's plans, which included several clever new names, they decided to become Dead Frog. "The name was shocking in a humorous way, and people remembered it."

Sales increased by 25 per cent within a few months after the name change. The beer was the same, but the carefully marketed image was totally different. The new logo featured a flattened green frog with Xs over its eyes. Slogans such as "There's more hops in a dead frog" and T-shirts with the slogan "My pad or yours?" appeared. "Our merchandise flew off the shelves," marketing director Chris Landsman remembered. "We even got an order from a high school team in the southern United States. It had a meet coming up against its archrivals, who had the word "frogs" in their nickname, and they wanted Dead Frog shirts to wear when they went to the other high school to compete."

The tremendous success of the marketing plan resulted in major changes for Dead Frog. The company needed a larger plant to keep up with growing demand and a bottling line that would make it possible for the product be distributed beyond the Lower Mainland. In the spring of 2008, the brewery moved to a nearly one-thousand-square-metre facility and expanded its staff to thirty people. The installation of a bottling line resulted in a 300 per cent jump in sales in just over six months. By 2009, the plant was producing eight thousand hectolitres of beer.

But trouble was brewing. Instead of using conventional brown long-neck bottles, Dead Frog decided on clear glass bottles embossed with the frog logo. "We wanted to create a premium image to show off our beers," Landsman said. Sleeman Brewery, a fiefdom in the multinational empire of Sapporo of Japan, took offence, claiming that the design of the Dead Frog bottle was a deliberate imitation of its own clear glass bottles. Smith decided to fight the (still unsettled) lawsuit brought on by Sleeman and the resulting newspaper stories, which portrayed Smith's brewery as a David fighting the Sapporo giant, generated considerable publicity and a great deal of sympathy for Dead Frog.

The zany marketing has certainly raised Dead Frog's profile among BC's beer drinkers, but it's the beers themselves that bring people back. "I create the beers I like," Smith remarked. "They're quality beers for discerning drinkers. They're neither mainstream nor wild and funky."

Dead Frog Lager is the closest of the four year-round brews to being mainstream. "We wanted it to be full-flavoured—not too light, but easy to drink. We used more malts than a Czech pilsner and made it less bitter," Smith explained. It's the brewery's top seller. Honey Lager is an effervescent, slightly more full-bodied beer than the lager, with subtle honey notes. "It was our first beer and it's undergone the most changes. At first it was an English-style ale, but we wanted it to be lighter, so we made it a lager."

Pale Ale, a light amber, medium-bodied ale, balances hop and malt flavours. "We don't pretend to be a West Coast-style pale ale; we don't want to overwhelm people with hops," Landsman commented. Nut Brown Ale, the second-best seller and a Canadian Brewing Awards gold medal winner is, he continued, "our pride and joy. There aren't many nut browns in BC so this increases our uniqueness as a brewery." Medium-bodied, it has strong notes of chocolate and espresso. "We didn't want it to be like most English browns, with little carbonation and quite heavy in body, so we lightened it up and increased the carbonation," Smith noted. The closest Dead Frog has come to the funky end of the spectrum was in the naming of the only limited edition beer it has created, a smooth amber ale that is humorously called 2½ Year Anniversary Ale.

Russell's head brewer, Jack Bensley, left a career as a high school
math and science teacher to become a professional brewer.

The employees of many microbreweries often say that they feel like
members of a family but since in 1995, when brothers Peter and Mark
Russell joined their father, Arthur, to start a brewery, Surrey's **Russell**

Brewing Company has literally been a family affair. The brewery initially produced two English-style ales, an amber and a cream, which were distributed on draft in Vancouver and the Lower Mainland, and built a small but enthusiastic following.

One of Russell's first and most devoted fans was Andrew Harris, owner of a Vancouver restaurant that was a steady customer. When the Russells decided to sell the business, they approached Harris. He, in turn, approached his father, Brian, who was considering retirement after several decades of setting up tech companies in such places as South Africa and Australia. In 2004, Russell Brewing became a Harris family business: Brian was the CEO, Andrew the COO, and his brothers Paul and P.J. and sister Angela the heads of the production, marketing, and sales divisions, respectively.

The Harris family soon decided to expand beyond Greater Vancouver to the Fraser Valley and areas north of Vancouver. In 2008, they raised their Vancouver profile by signing an exclusivity agreement with the BC Lions professional football club to sell BC Lions Lager at BC Place. "They'd been doing business with Molson," Paul Harris remembered, "and we came to the table as small fish. But they were impressed by our passion and energy." In addition to the lager they created for football fans, they moved beyond the two English ales that they'd been brewing since they'd assumed ownership. "We wanted to offer a larger range of styles at a variety of prices."

Three purchases developed Russell Brewing's profile and market share: Fort Garry Brewing Company of Winnipeg in 2007, a canning line in 2008, and a bottling line a year later. "The acquisition of Fort Garry allowed us to expand eastward into Alberta and Manitoba," Harris said. "And having cans and bottles made it possible to offer our beers in liquor stores. Thirty per cent of our sales are now in packaged form, and we're aiming for a fifty-fifty split." Production grew so much that the company had to acquire a six-hundred-and-fifty-square-metre warehouse for storing the packaged beer. In 2010, production had reached ten thousand hectolitres a year and the number of employees had expanded to forty.

Head brewer Jack Bensley, a long-time homebrewer who left his job as a high school math and physics teacher to begin studying for a Master's degree in brewing and distilling from Scotland's Heriot-Watt

University, described Russell as a craft brewery that filled a variety of niches. "Approachable craft beer is the basis of Russell. We have a range of styles designed to appeal to entry-level and more experienced tastes. We're unusual among microbreweries because we have four lagers." He described BC Lions as a fairly mainstream type of lager, light-bodied, with a subdued malt profile. Rocky Mountain Pilsner is designed as a "better entry-level beer" that is much hoppier than mainstream lagers and has a "bit of an edge." Extra Special Lager is a premium beer, more full-bodied than Rocky Mountain, and, at 5.5 per cent ABV, stronger than the other two. Lime Lager is a popular, fruit-flavoured summer beer that is brewed with some wheat malt to give it greater clarity and a longer-lasting white head.

Russell's three year-round ales reflect its commitment to maintaining the English ales tradition upon which the brewery established its early reputation. Honey Blonde Ale, which Bensley described as like an English golden ale, is a mild, smooth-drinking, summer beer with understated honey notes. Russell Pale Ale is also in the English style, with a gentle balance of hop and malt flavours. Cream Ale, the brewery's flagship product, is "like an English mild, darker and maltier than North American examples" of the style. It's medium-bodied, with coffee and caramel notes.

The popularity of these ales and lagers has, Bensley remarked happily, "given me the opportunity to play." In late 2009, he began brewing a number of limited releases under the label the Brewmaster Series. Packaged in 650-millilitre bottles, these have included IP'eh!, which introduced three types of hops during the boiling phase of the brewing and another during the fermentation stage. "It's close to my heart," Bensley enthused about his 6.5 per cent ABV creation. Black Death Porter, another in the series, is a very dark, full-bodied ale in the "wee heavy" Scottish tradition. As it is also 6.5 per cent ABV, drinking it may result, the advertising copy warns, "in excessive laughter or brutal honesty."

❖

When a top executive in the Insurance Corporation of British Columbia suggested that Darryll Frost open a brewpub on the ground floor of Surrey's new Central City Tower, Frost quickly agreed. He liked the

Gary Lohin, brewmaster at Central City, stands beside a poster
for the Red Racer line of beers. Both the illustration of the
girl riding the bike and the name have caused controversy.

demographics of the rapidly expanding city twenty kilometres south of
Vancouver. The brewery would be next to a large shopping mall and a
hundred or so metres away from the southernmost station of the SkyTrain.
More important, officials explained to him, Central City Tower would be
filled with the offices of ICBC and other companies, all of whose employees
would become frequent patrons. Frost gathered together twenty investors
and developed a five-million-dollar, twelve-hundred-square-metre brewpub, **Central City Brewing Company**.

After Central City Brewing opened in 2004, things didn't go as well
as planned. The Central City Tower offices remained almost empty; in
fact, the facility didn't become fully occupied until 2009 when Simon
Fraser University opened its Surrey Campus. "We really depended on
sales from our liquor store," Frost commented, referring to the retail
outlet that had been moved from the brewpub complex to the shopping
mall next door, where it quickly became one of the province's leading
stores in volume of sales.

"We've changed and developed a great deal. For example, our restaurant has become a gastropub. We're constantly working on creating imaginative ways of cooking local foods," remarked Frost, who received formal training as a chef in England and worked for many years with the Mark James Group of restaurants in the Vancouver area. The other major development was in the brewing department, which evolved into a rapidly growing microbrewery. By 2009, packaged beer accounted for 90 per cent of sales.

Since Central City's inception, the beer has been the responsibility of Gary Lohin, whose parents once gave him a homebrew starter kit. "It was for Coopers Real Ale," he recalled. He began his professional training at Okanagan Spring in Vernon, where "I learned how very important cleanliness was." He became the initial brewer at North Vancouver's Sailor Hagar's, Greater Vancouver area's first brewpub. "That's when I first got to brew what I wanted. I liked hops and had fun playing with IPAs and an ESB."

"I was given a free hand when I joined Central City," Lohin said. "We started up with a hoppy beer and a darker one and, when the response was positive, we began offering several lesser-known styles, including a Belgian *tripel* and a barley wine." Other special brews included Boomer's Red Ale, Steelhead Stout, Iceberg Copper Bock, and an Imperial IPA. The various styles were popular not only in the brewpub, but also in the liquor store, where they were sold in bottles.

The breakthrough came when Central City decided to install a canning line capable of filling twelve thousand cans an hour and later to package their most popular styles under the brand name Red Racer. "Some of our people had seen and admired a painting by a local artist showing a girl in a skirt riding a mid-twentieth-century bicycle. He agreed to let us use it in our label designs." The new canned product sold exceptionally well. In 2010, the brewery produced eight thousand hectolires, double the previous year's output.

The Red Racer label became the subject of ongoing controversy. Initially, provincial government officials objected to the fact that the wind had blown back the rider's skirt, exposing her right thigh and a garter holding up one of her silk stockings. Brewery executives convinced the government that there were other, far more risqué labels on the market. Then, in the fall of 2009, the Bear Republic Brewing Company of

California sent Central City a "cease and desist" letter, claiming that the Red Racer labels violated its own copyrighted designs and names. Noting that Red Racer is packaged in cans while Bear Brewing Company's products are bottled, that the designs are markedly different, and that Bear's products are called "Racer 5" and "Red Rocket Ale," Central City rejected the claim. In 2010, a court in Massachusetts, where the California brewer had filed suit, ruled in favour of Central City.

Five Red Racer beers are available throughout the year. The Bavarian-style Red Racer Lager uses a pilsen malt to give the beer a pale colour and a flavour that doesn't overpower the hops. Light-bodied and crisp, it is the top seller at the brewpub. IPA, the best seller in cans, has been listed as the third-best beer in Canada by the consumer group Beer Advocate. Five different hops are used in the brewing process, providing floral aromas, a citrusy flavour, and a bitterness level of over eighty. "But," Lohin says, "the malts make the difference, giving a smooth, medium body." At 6.5 per cent ABV, it is the strongest of Central City's canned products. Red Racer Pale Ale is much maltier than the IPA. "We use English Maris Otter malts, an English-style malt noted for the rich flavour it gives ales; they are big and generous malts that back up the hops. You experience the sweetness of the malts first and then the Golding hops. I like to say that our pale ale has an English flavour with a West Coast zing." Wheat Ale, a Belgian-style ale, is straw-coloured and unfiltered. It has notes of coriander and orange, and is lighter bodied and more carbonated than the other three. ESB, the most recent addition to the list, is a traditional English bitter.

Both Lohin and Frost spoke enthusiastically about the future of Central City Brewing and the possibility of soon opening a much larger brewery. With the present plant working at maximum capacity, Central City is barely keeping up with the growing demand. Lohin noted, "With a new plant, we could install a new bottling line for limited edition brews. My goal is to make our beers a point of difference in the market. Successful brewers have to keep pushing, experimenting; they have to come up with something different."

Of the future, Frost noted, "We want to be known as *the* craft brewer in BC and maybe all of the country. We don't want to be number two. We are already test marketing in Boston and St. Louis. We want to make more beer—properly. Some places increase the volume by rushing the

Surrey's Big Ridge Brewing exhibits posters of its main brands on the restaurant walls.

process. We want to make sure that we take the necessary time to produce a very good beer. That's what Sierra Nevada and New Belgium did in the United States. They produce a great deal of beer, but they're still craft brewers."

❖

When it was founded in 1999, **Big Ridge Brewing Company** of Surrey was at the edge of what was then a largely rural, agricultural area north of the international border. Over the next decade, subdivisions and shopping centres were developed, and the brewpub's business grew too large for the building it occupied in a shopping centre nestled at the base of Panorama Ridge. In the spring of 2010, Big Ridge moved across the road and two blocks east. The new restaurant seats a hundred and fifty and the pub a hundred. Two buildings away stands the Big Ridge Liquor Store.

Although it's one of four brewpubs owned by the Mark James Group, it isn't a cookie-cutter version of the other three. "The ownership intended each restaurant to be part of the area in which it's located, developing its own menus and beers. For example, here we feature several Chinese dishes that aren't found in the other three. And each brewer has his own approach to the beers he creates," Chris Funk, the manager, commented. Since 2008, Tariq Khan has been Big Ridge's brewer. A native of Montreal, he earned a diploma in brewing at the University of Sunderland in England and worked at English breweries before moving to BC. "English styles are my heart and soul," he said, but added that he enjoyed the freedom that working at a brewpub gave him. "I've had a chance to develop some German lagers and Belgian ales, something I never could have done if I'd stayed in England."

It's not surprising that, situated as it is in a newer suburban area that had been predominantly rural, the brewery's largest seller is lager. Called Harvest Lager in honour of South Surrey's agricultural heritage, it's a crossover beer. "When people order a Bud," Funk remarked, "we offer them a taste of our lager." Khan described it as an easy-drinking, North American pale lager. "It's highly carbonated and has more pro-nounced malt than hop notes. But it isn't too challenging for people who like mainstream beers." Rodeo Red, named after an annual event held in nearby Cloverdale, is an English amber that uses English spe-cialty malts. "It marks the next stage in the evolution from mainstream to craft-beer drinker." Chimney Hill Wheat, named for a local area, blends fruit and clove notes. Like most wheat beers, it's lightly hopped and offers a rich, chewy, bready flavour. It is more highly carbonated than many examples of the style, a feature designed to make it more appealing to crossover drinkers.

Old Sullivan Porter and Clover Ale, Big Ridge's other two core beers, are solidly in the English tradition. As Khan described it, the former is "roasty and chocolatey, with hints of peat smoke. Aging it with oak spirals gives it a distinctive flavour. It has a creamy, smooth texture." The latter, a West Coast-style India pale ale is, at 6 per cent ABV, the most potent of the five beers and also the most assertive in flavour, with plenty of hops.

❖

Turning Point Brewery is just over a hundred metres from the Fraser River on Annacis Island in Delta. A subsidiary of the Mark Anthony Group, whose products include Mike's Hard Lemonade and Mission Hill

Wines, Turning Point Brewery came into being when Molson acquired the western Canadian distribution rights for Corona, once a major part of the Mark Anthony portfolio. With a sales network in place, but without Corona to sell, the company decided to enter the brewing business.

It started with two value-priced beers, Hell's Gate Lager, a fairly mainstream lager, and, Hell's Gate Pale Ale, a lightly hopped pale ale, both available in cans and on draft. In 2009, Turning Point began to produce a premium beer under the Stanley Park Brewing Company name. Stanley Park 1897 Amber Ale is described as a Belgian-style beer that was inspired by Frank Foubert, a Belgian who, late in the nineteenth century, opened a brewery near the entrance to Canada's most famous urban park. Packaged in custom-designed bottles, the beer was announced as the first of "The Founder's Series."

❖

Big River Brew Pub, less than half a kilometre from the Fraser River, is part of the Riverport Sports and Entertainment Complex, which was established a kilometre east of Highway 99 to serve the rapidly growing city of Richmond. When Chuck Wills opened the brewpub in 1998, its only neighbour was the SilverCity multiplex cinema. Since then, several new businesses have been established, including aquatic, basketball, and ice-skating centres, a Gold's Gym, and the Zone Bowling Centre, which is in the same building as Big River.

Although several fast-food outlets and a Spaghetti Factory restaurant have also opened, the brewpub and accompanying restaurant dominate the eating scene. Movie patrons come by before or after they've been to the multiplex. "When *Avatar* was showing during the Christmas season in 2009, we had a big run on our most popular beers," brewmaster Damon Robson remarked.

Robson, who earned a degree in chemistry at the University of Exeter in England, came to Canada in 1994. His first jobs were in construction and, after work, he found himself drinking mainstream domestic lagers. "They were terrible," he recalled. "It was time to put my university training to practical use." He started at Whistler Brewing Company, where his co-workers included such future award-winning brewers as Mike Kelly (Nelson Brewing) and Matt Phillips (Phillips Brewing), then moved

BIG RIV

BREWING CO.

0 mL   Handcrafted Ales & Lag

BREWED & BOTTLED BY BIG RIVER B

www.bigriverbrewpub.com · Richmond,

With a degree in chemistry, including what he calls "beer applications,"
from the University of Exeter, Big River brewmaster Damon Robson decided
he should put his formal training to use shortly after he moved to Canada.

briefly to Brewsters Brewpub in Lethbridge, and arrived at Big River in
2001. "Working at a brewpub presents a different set of challenges than
working at a microbrewery. At a microbrewery, you're part of a team working together to create beer. Here it's all on you. You can use your individual
creativity, but you have to take sole responsibility for the result."

In talking about the beers he brews for Big River, Robson referred to his English background, which not only influenced the styles but also governed his philosophy about drinking in a brewpub. "I don't want our beers to be too extreme. They should be session beers, easy to drink, not too filling, not too strong, not too carbonated. They should be sociable, something you can enjoy with friends sitting around a table at the local."

Big River Pilsner and Vienna Lager are the brewpub's top sellers. The former is a Bohemian-style pilsner, with a fuller malt taste than is often found in the style. The latter is copper-coloured and dominated by the malts, with some fruitiness supplied by the hops. Blonde Ale, slightly effervescent with a sweet finish, was designed, Robson explained, "to wean people from mainstream lagers" like the ones he had to drink during his first year in Canada.

Pale Ale and Extra Special Bitter reflect Robson's English roots. "I grew up with British pales; I find the West Coast style of pale ale too hoppy. We use caramel malts to create a balance with the hop flavours. You don't get the residual bitterness. Like the beers I grew up with, it's low in carbonation." About the bitter, he enthused, "It hits my taste buds. The Cascade hops give notes of grapefruit but malts make it less bitter than the Pale Ale." Two darker beers round out Big River's regular offerings: the medium-bodied Nut Brown Ale has hints of toffee, burnt caramel, and chocolate; Robson described the Stout as "sweeter and thicker than Guinness. It walks the line between a dry and a sweet stout."

Old Yale Brewing Company
    5616 Vedder Rd, Chilliwack, V2R 3M7, 604-858-2537
    oldyalebrewingcompany.com
Mission Springs Brewing Company
    7160 Oliver St, Mission, V2V 6K5, 604-820-1009
    missionspringsbrewingcompany.com
Dead Frog Brewery
    1 - 27272 Gloucester Way, Aldergrove, V4W 4A1, 604-856-1055, deadfrog.ca
Russell Brewing Company
    202 - 13018 80th Ave, Surrey, V3W 3A8, 604-599-1190, russellbeer.com
Central City Brewing Company
    13450 102 Ave, Central City Mall, Surrey, V3T 5X3, 604-582-6620
    centralcitybrewing.com

Big Ridge Brewing Company
  5580 152 St, Surrey, V3S 9A5, 604-574-2739, markjamesgroup.com
Turning Point Brewery
  465 Fraserview Pl, Delta, V3M 6H4, 604-519-5370, turningpointbrewery.com
Big River Brew Pub
  140 – 14200 Entertainment Way, Richmond, V6W 1K2, 604-271-2739, zbowl.com

CHAPTER SEVEN

Beyond Molson Coors
A Vancouver Circ-Ale Tour

Since it opened in 1953 as Capilano Brewery, **Molson Coors'** Vancouver brewery, just beyond the west end of Vancouver's Burrard Street Bridge, has dominated Vancouver's beer scene. An enormous complex occupying more than two city blocks, it is the largest brewery west of Toronto, employing two hundred and twenty people and annually brewing 1.8 million hectolitres. In it are produced the company's two largest-selling beers, Molson Canadian and Coors Light, along with Miller Genuine Draft, Rickard's Red, Old Style Pilsner, Black Label, and, only for export to the United States, Japan's Asahi beer.

In 1984, when Granville Island Brewing opened a few blocks to the east, Vancouver's beer scene began to change. Now, a quarter of a century later, it is possible to leave the Molson parking lot and make a ten-kilometre circle tour, visiting three brewpubs and three microbreweries before returning to the giant brewery.

❖

Yaletown Brewing Company, Vancouver's oldest brewpub, was established in 1994 in what had been an aging warehouse district. During the early 1990s, when plans to transform the neighbourhood into a trendy centre of high-end shops, restaurants, and residences, Mark James, the owner of an upscale restaurant and fashionable clothing store in Vancouver's Kitsilano area, took notice. Yaletown was fairly close to BC Place and GM Place (the homes, respectively, of the BC Lions professional football club and the Vancouver Canucks hockey club) and to a station for the small ferries that delivered passengers across False Creek to Granville Island.

James renovated an eighty-four-year-old building that had been, among other things, a warehouse and a laundry. The original beams were retained, an antique fireplace was brought in from Mexico, 1880s cast-iron railings from England were installed, and tiles from France and hardwood flooring from an old Victoria hotel were laid. A pool table and

Opened in 1953 as Capilano Brewery, the Molson Coors
Vancouver plant is the largest brewery west of Toronto.

dart board helped to create an English pub atmosphere. The renovated
building was divided into pub and restaurant areas, and a street-side
patio was added.

Iain Hill, the co-ordinating brewer for the four Mark James brewpubs,
has been the brewmaster for Yaletown since its opening. A biochemistry
graduate of the University of Victoria who didn't know what an ESB
(extra special bitter) was when his homebrewing father first took him to
Victoria's Spinnakers Gastro Brewpub, he became the weekend brewer
for Shaftebury, one of Vancouver's early microbreweries. "I worked on
Friday nights when nobody else wanted to."

Yaletown's beer list consists of six year-round offerings and a wide
variety of seasonals. "All of our beers are unfiltered," Hill noted. "We
vary serving temperatures from five degrees Celsius for our lagers and
wheat beers to ten degrees for our darker beers." Mainland Lager,
although a light-bodied, straw-coloured North American-style beer, is
brewed with Czech hops and, while it is more hoppy than malty, it has
fuller malt flavours than mainstream lagers. Hill's Special Wheat is a
traditional German *hefeweizen*. A cloudy beer, its spicy and fruity notes
give it a refreshing finish. "It's one of the most difficult beers I brew,"
Hill remarked. "The yeasts are very finicky."

Tariq Khan (left), brewmaster at Big Ridge, and Iain Hill, co-ordinating brewer for the four Mark James brewpubs, relax in front of the equipment at Yaletown Brewing.

Brick & Beam IPA (a reference to the brewpub's interior decoration) and Nagila Pale Ale (from the Yiddish word for "rejoice") are both West Coast-style ales. The former, at sixty IBUs, is strongly hopped. "But it's smooth for an IPA, with malt flavours balancing the citrus notes." Hill refers to the latter as "a palate cleaner," and described the impact of the hops as "like an elastic band going off in your mouth." Downtown Brown, one of the two regular dark beers, is rich in malts and has coffee notes. Warehouse Stout is a dry stout. Both are nitrogen-infused "to smooth out the rough edges."

The names of several of these beers, all solid and familiar favourites among craft-beer aficionados, link them to the establishment and to the neighbourhood. The names for Hill's seasonal and special edition beers are more unusual, as befits the brews themselves: Le Nez Rouge, Leopard Ale, Mélange à Trois, and Jolly Hooligan, to name but four. The last in the list isn't Irish, as the name might suggest, but a Belgian *dubbel* ale, one of several of Hill's creations that follow such somewhat unfamiliar Belgian styles. One of the most interesting is Oud Bruin, a sweet-and-sour Flemish ale that is brewed with four different yeasts and aged for a year in oak barrels. "It's probably the only one in Canada and one of the few in North America," Hill stated, a note of pride in his voice.

❖❖

Steamworks Brewing Company is eight blocks north of Yaletown, located where Water Street meets Cordova. It's on the edge of Gastown, another formerly run-down area that has been transformed into a "historical" district. Steamworks offers the most spectacular views of any brewpub in western Canada. Looking from the patio or out of the glass windows that line the north side of the pub, patrons can view Burrard Inlet and beyond that the North Shore mountains. Art galleries, clothing boutiques, and fashionable stores line the street to the south. With stations for Vancouver's SkyTrain and SeaBus close by, the restaurant and pub are easily reached not just by professionals from nearby office buildings or tourists staying in nearby hotels, but also by people from all over Greater Vancouver.

Established in 1995 in a century-old building that had been a warehouse, Steamworks is divided into two floors. The main floor and its adjacent patio offer the expansive views; the lower floor, reached by a spiral staircase, contains a restaurant and bar, behind which are displayed the brewery's mash tun, brew kettle, and three fermenters. This floor also has the building's original wood beams, posts, and cement flooring. A historic steam pipe, which runs beneath Gastown's buildings, gives the

Steamworks, one of the most popular destinations in Vancouver's popular Gastown district, offers good food and beer and great views of Burrard Inlet and the North Shore mountains.

pub its name; it is visible in the downstairs women's washroom and is used to heat the brew kettles.

"We feature good food at reasonable prices," manager Kirsten Delbeke said, noting the prominence that wild BC salmon enjoys on the menu. "But what makes us more than just another good Gastown restaurant is the fact that we brew our own beer."

Conrad Gmoser has been in charge of brewing that beer almost since Steamworks opened. After graduating with a degree in architecture from Montreal's McGill University, he began an internship in Vancouver with a firm that was handling the renovations of the building that would become the brewpub. "One of the partners of the firm was also a co-owner of the new brewpub, and, when things were slow at the office, I was assigned to the crew doing the actual renovations. I'd been a homebrewer and was interested in how brewers Shirley Warne and Harley Smith were setting things up. I would sometimes help on a part-time basis and, in 1996, when they both became involved in other projects, I became the head brewer."

Lions Gate Lager, Steamworks' top-selling brew, is, according to the website description "Vancouver's gateway to flavour." "I wanted a balanced, drinkable session beer," Gmoser commented, "a beer that's not North American, but one that a North American lager drinker would enjoy." He created a German *helles* (the word means "pale" or "bright" in German) using traditional German lager yeasts and Saaz hops. Light-bodied and highly carbonated, the beer is crisp and clean finishing. Signature Pale Ale, the second-best seller, designed to be a beer that "won't knock the socks off a lager drinker," is an English-style ale with fewer hops than its West Coast cousin. It is copper in colour and its caramel malts balance the hop notes. To Gmoser, Ipanema Summer White Ale, a Belgian-style wheat beer, is special. "I first tasted wheat beer when I was eighteen years old and travelling in Germany. Ever since then, it's been a Holy Grail quest for me to make a good wheat beer." Brewed with barley and oats as well as wheat, Ipanema is cloudy, fruity, and spicy, using orange peel and coriander flavourings.

If the lager, pale ale, and wheat beer are designed to bring inexperienced craft-beer drinkers into the fold, Gmoser's other beers are for the more experienced and, to a degree, adventurous drinkers. They are fuller in body and flavour and often darker in colour. Nirvana Nut Brown Ale is malty, low in carbonation, and moderately hopped. Empress IPA is, by contrast, well-hopped. "The favourite beer of our regulars," it is fairly bitter, but has herbal and fruity characteristics as well. Cole Porter uses chocolate malts to create a creamy chocolate finish with some hop notes, while Heroic Stout has a roasty bitterness. Among the more interesting limited edition beers Gmoser has created are those featuring such additives as raspberry and watermelon.

Summing up the beers he's designed, the one-time architecture student commented, "In our regular beers I like to keep a balance between hops and malts. But for our seasonal beers, I'm eclectic. I enjoy experimenting. My raspberry beer was 9 per cent ABV, with a pound of raspberries per gallon. I wasn't looking for balance there."

Three kilometres east of Steamworks, where Water Street, now turned into Powell, crosses Commercial Drive, stands **Storm Brewing Limited**, in a gritty neighbourhood where the women standing on the corner aren't waiting for the light to change. The entrance to the brewery is from an

James Walton of Storm Brewery, Vancouver's smallest microbrewery, has been referred to by fellow brewers as "Captain Qwirk," a reference to his unusual marketing methods.

alley beside a loading dock and is indicated only by a small sign hanging over the door. The brewing equipment is at the back of a small room organized in a style that could be called creative chaos.

Owner-brewer-salesman James Walton began making beer as a young teenager in Port Alberni on Vancouver Island, and, when a beer strike hit the area in the late 1970s, he found that his homebrewing hobby was greatly appreciated by his father's friends. It wasn't until a decade and a half later, after earning a degree in mycology (the study of fungi), unsuccessfully operating a mushroom farm, and working for a large pharmaceutical company, that he turned his hobby into a profession. "I remember going to Seattle, seeing all the microbreweries there, and thinking, 'Wow! They're homebrewing at a professional level!' I knew that's what I wanted to do."

He took an old boiler from the pharmaceutical company he worked for—"It was my severance pay," he joked—scrounged two large tubs from a scrap yard—"I think one had been used for making yogurt"—acquired brewing space in what used to be the headquarters of a Chinese food wholesaler, and then used his skills as a welder to set up a small brewing system. In 1995, he opened his brewery. "I've always liked being an entrepreneur. Beer is my art form, and I can use my training as a scientist."

Red Sky Alt, the first beer he created, came on the market in June 1995. It was based on a complex and infrequently brewed German style. "It's a very complicated style. I wanted to start with a good beer that has complexity. But it was too complex and very difficult to make. The recipe included five hops and six malts. I don't make it anymore." Walton had created a good beer, but it wasn't easy to sell his product. "People thought that I was some homebrewer, and they used to ask me if I had a licence."

The *alt* was followed by a porter and a wheat beer, which, like all his beers, are sold on draft only to Vancouver-area restaurants and bars. Strong in alcohol (only four of the eighteen beers he has brewed have been under 6 per cent ABV), pushing the styles to the limits, the beers quickly developed a small but loyal following among Walton's two sets of target drinkers: people who have a palate for good food and like drinks that enhance their food, and beer geeks.

He has also earned a reputation as, what fellow craft brewer Barry Benson of R&B Brewing called, "Captain Qwirk." Noted Canadian beer writer Stephen Beaumont described one of his brews as "on the edge of being totally out of control," a statement proudly displayed on Storm Brewing's web page. Walton has referred to himself as "the evil genius." Part of this reputation was created by his unusual branding and marketing. His stout, for example, was called Black Plague and the tap handles dispensing it were adorned with rubber rats. Other beers have been named after types of storms: Hail Stone, Hurricane, Ice Storm, Precipitation, and Stiff Breeze. Some of his beers have used such uncommon additives as basil and ginseng. He even brewed a beer using echinacea, a daisy-like plant to which practitioners of folk medicine attribute healing properties.

Hurricane IPA, Walton's top seller, is in the English tradition of the later nineteenth century, although he said that he preferred not to limit his creations by affixing style names to them. He referred to it as "a session IPA," even though it checks in at between 6 and 7 per cent ABV. Someone drinking it, he reported, should first notice the fruity aromas, then taste the yeast and the sweetness of malt, followed by a bitterness from the hops during the swallow. At 8 per cent ABV, Black Plague Stout is even stronger. "I started out trying to make an Irish dry stout, a kind of Guinness for Vancouver. But I soon changed that. You'll first experience coffee, taffy, and raisin aromas. Then you'll get some sweetness from the malts and after, a dry bitterness. You can taste the alcohol in it; one winter it went up to 11 per cent. It ain't Guinness. I'm really proud of this beer."

Storm Brewing's two other regular offerings are each 5 per cent ABV. Regarding Highland Scottish Ale, Walton commented, "I've made over 800 batches of it, so by now I guess I know how to do it." He credits the inspiration for the beer to his friend, punk rocker David "Malty" Macanulty, who, he said, is very difficult to please. The peat-smoked malt he uses can be detected in the aroma and first sips. It's mildly hopped, and its main feature is the complexity of the malt flavours. Precipitation Pilsner, which "doesn't really represent the brewery," was created at the request of his customers who faced the challenge of providing something for their mainstream lager drinkers. Its crispness comes from the Saaz hops, while the malts provide a slight sweetness. "It has that 'lager socks' smell," he laughed, referring to an aroma that old-style north German beers used to have.

Walton referred to his three Belgian *lambic* beers as "one of my crazy ideas, a way of expressing my creativity." Complex and sour, they are aged for at least a year in oak barrels. The fruit—raspberry, blackberry, or black cherry—provides a secondary fermentation. "Some of them are still aging," he reported in the spring of 2010. "I've got five barrels left."

❖❖❖

Like Storm, R&B Brewing Company, three kilometres southeast, is in a gritty neighbourhood; Brewery Creek was named after several breweries that operated there during the late nineteenth and early twentieth century. Much like Storm, it's cramped and crowded, with production facilities and offices squeezed into just over two hundred and eighty square metres of space. However, there are differences. R&B annually produces three thousand hectolitres compared to Storm's fifteen hundred, and employs nine workers to Storm's two. In addition to distributing on draft, it also packages six of its brews in 650-millilitre bottles.

Rick Dellow, along with partner Barry Benson, worked for Molson and for Newlands Systems, a beer-equipment company, before starting R&B in 1997.

Friends for over two decades, R&B's founders Rick Dellow and Barry Benson come from different brewing backgrounds. The former trained at the brewing school of Heriot-Watt University in Edinburgh and worked for British brewing giants Whitbread and Bass before coming to Canada. The latter studied Food Science at the British Columbia Institute of Technology and then brewing at Chicago's Siebel Institute before joining Shaftebury, one of BC's early microbreweries. The two, who got to know each other while working for Molson in Vancouver, joined Newlands Systems of Abbotsford, BC, a fabricator and installer of brewing systems, after Molson merged with Carling-O'Keefe in 1989, and then travelled around the world for the company, setting up breweries and training staff.

Dellow and Benson had always wanted to own and operate their own brewery. At this time, Storm, Granville Island, and Russell operated in the Vancouver area. "But we felt there was room for us," Dellow said. "It took us two years to raise the money and four or five months to set up the brewery. Our first beer, Red Devil, an English-style red ale, came out in November 1997."

To get their product known, the partners visited a lot of restaurants and bars, sponsored tastings, attended beer festivals, and held a series of tasting seminars to educate restaurant servers about various styles, helping them to notice imperfections in various brews. Referring to R&B's unofficial motto, "Fun and Profit," Dellow agreed that everyone had a lot of fun in the early years, but it was five years before the brewery became self-sustaining.

Before describing R&B's beers, Dellow noted that they are designed for younger drinkers interested in pairing flavourful beers with good food, middle-aged beer nerds, and old-timers who remember, or think they remember, how good beer used to be.

With two exceptions, the beers are in the British tradition. Red Devil, which has gradually evolved into a traditional English pale ale, is coppery-red in colour and emphasizes a balance between the malts and three types of hops, each of which is introduced at a different stage of the brewing process. Hoppelganger IPA, at 6 per cent ABV, is R&B's strongest product and could be called a hybrid between English and West Coast styles. Although it registers at forty-five IBUs, the hops do not overwhelm. There are floral and grapefruit notes, and a slightly sweet finish. Raven Cream Ale, a 4.8 per cent ABV English dark mild and R&B's top seller, is a light-bodied beverage with smoky and nutty flavours. Dark Star Oatmeal Stout offers chocolate and coffee flavours, with a slight bitterness. The carbonation, higher than in many stouts, gives it a lighter body and mouth-feel. Each of these ales is distinguished by a very clean

finish, a characteristic Dellow attributes to the strains of yeast (which he did not identify) used. Each of these beers is available in bottles.

Sun God Wheat Ale, also in bottles, is a North American-style *kristalweizen*, a filtered, light-bodied, straw-coloured beer. "When we introduced it, we didn't think that Vancouver was ready for an unfiltered, cloudy *hefeweizen*. It has a cereal flavour and is dry and crisp." Bohemian Lager was, Dellow noted, named to describe both the Czech style of the beer and the personalities of the people who worked in the brewery. "We only started to brew it because our customers requested a lager. But it's been a real success." The hops give the gold-coloured brew a clean, dry, finish, while the malts provide a more robust flavour and a medium body. "Finally," the web page description of the beer notes, "a real lager for the beer nerd in all of us."

Just before and during the 2010 Vancouver Winter Olympics, Bohemian underwent two changes. The beer remained the same, but for a short while it was available in 650-millilitre bottles. The brewers also gave it a new name: Iceholes Celebration Lager. Like other local breweries, R&B had wanted to be involved with the 2010 Winter Olympics, but Molson held the beer rights and the Vancouver Olympic Committee jealously guarded the Games' official names and logos. Then, when American television comic Steven Colbert, during a humorous rant about perceived injustices against the American speed-skating team, called Canadians a bunch of "syrup sucking ice holes," the brewery had its opportunity. It renamed and bottled the lager, and printed up posters for display at drinking establishments. "So someone thinks we're Iceholes?" the poster asked. "Well, don't get mad, get even . . . Wreak your revenge in a very Canadian way, have a beer!" Dellow smiled as he announced that Bohemian/Iceholes was R&B's top seller during the Olympics.

❖

Dockside Restaurant and Brewing Company is two and a half kilometres west of R&B, on the eastern tip of Granville Island, another Vancouver area that has been transformed into a fashionable district. Part of the Granville Island Hotel, it opened in 1997 as The Creek Brewery. The pub, restaurant, and patio look out on False Creek and beyond, to the Vancouver skyline to the north and to posh condos to the south.

Daniel Knibbs, brewmaster at Dockside Restaurant and
Brewing Company, worked for several breweries as a volunteer
and part-time assistant before assuming his present position.

Rowboats, pleasure boats, and small water taxis ply the waters. The
brewpub appeals to day trippers to the island, hotel guests, students
from nearby Emily Carr University of Art + Design, and, in increasing
numbers, members of the local craft-beer crowd.

Daniel Knibbs, brewmaster since early 2010, jokingly described himself as "your typical Alberta beer connoisseur—Big Rock, Boddingtons,
and Guinness." That is, until he met Storm Brewing's James Walton.
"I tried his IPA and that pushed the 'on' button. I began to educate my
palate." He attended and volunteered at beer events, worked part-time
in an upscale liquor store, homebrewed, and helped out at Storm and
at the Yaletown, Taylor's Crossing, and Mission Springs brewpubs. After
serving two years as part-time "wort master" at Dead Frog, he came to
Dockside.

Since Dockside's inception, its core beer list has been dominated by
German styles. The current menu includes five lagers and a *hefeweizen*,
along with a pale and a brown ale. Marina Light Lager, created for consumers of mainstream products, is sweet and highly carbonated. Johnston

Street Pilsner balances malts and hops, while Old Bridge Dark Lager is a Vienna-style amber beer that has more malts than the pilsner. Jamaican Lager is a sweet and slightly pink-hued fruit beer that includes hibiscus concentrate. Like Alder Bay Honey Lager, it is a very popular summer beer. Haupenthal's Hefeweizen is unfiltered and features yeasty notes.

Cartwright is a West Coast-style pale ale that uses whole hop flowers to emphasize the flavours and aromas of the Cascade and Willamette Valley hops. Smooth and balanced, it is less bitter than most examples of the style. "I've brewed it to be people's introduction to the wonderful things hops can do for a beer," Knibbs enthused. Pelican Bay Brown is an English-style, low-carbonated beer to which the malts impart coffee and chocolate notes. And, as an expression of the brewer's love of hops, it has a noticeable hop finish.

Although he is at the beginning of his full-time career, Knibbs has a clear sense of what he wants to do as a brewer. "I want to bring palates on board and please those who are already on board. The beers should be true to style, drinkable, and food-worthy, for novices and beer geeks. I'll start taking baby steps with the recipes to bring them up to style."

❖

Granville Island Brewing Company, Canada's longest-operating micro-brewery, is a five-minute walk west from the Granville Island Hotel and a ten-minute walk east from Molson. From the outside, it looks pretty much as it did when it opened in June 1984, but inside, the brewery is very different. The production facilities now occupy a much smaller space than they originally did, and the cold beer store stocks a much wider selection of Granville Island brews. These changes are symbolic of the larger changes that have taken place.

The company has had several different owners. In 1985, Quantum Energy purchased a majority interest from founder Mitch Taylor and his partners. Then, in 1989, International Potter Distilling bought the brewery, along with Kelowna-based Calona Wines. That company went through a variety of ownership groups and, in 2009, sold the brewing business to Creemore Springs Brewery, a subsidiary of Molson Coors.

During the first decade, sales grew steadily, and the brewing system could not meet the increased demands for the product. In 1993, most

Vern Lambourne uses his wife's food processer to grind fresh ginger root he has just purchased at the Granville Island Public Market. It will become an essential ingredient in one of the Limited Edition beers he creates for Granville Island Brewing Company.

of the brewing began taking place in the large Kelowna building that also housed the winery, and the original facility started being used for the production of special release, Limited Edition brews. By the beginning of 2010, Granville Island Brewing's total annual production exceeded sixty-five thousand hectolitres, of which just under a thousand came from the brewery on Granville Island. In the spring of 2010, a third production location was added: Granville Island Lager and English Bay Pale Ale, the sales leaders, began to be brewed at the Molson Coors facility just west of the Burrard Street Bridge. The lager that was introduced to give Vancouverites an alternative to mainstream Canadian lagers is now produced in a plant run by one of Canada's two major producers of those very lagers.

Vern Lambourne, a biochemistry major at the University of Victoria and a "bit of a homebrewer" who wanted to enter the wine-making profession, is now in his tenth year as Granville Island's brewmaster, "The opportunities in the wine business were very limited," he recalled. "So I went to England and found a job in a brewpub." Here, he learned about creating beers in a variety of traditional British styles and about making sure that they had "sessionability," a smoothness that allowed the drinker to enjoy more than just one during an evening at the pub.

"The fact that I had an opportunity to learn about a wide range of styles and to get direct feedback from the customers certainly helped me when I returned to Canada." Back home, he worked at Steamworks, Mission Springs, and Big River brewpubs before taking over at Granville Island.

Lambourne, Joe Goetz, who ran brewing operations in Kelowna until 2009, and general manager Walter Cosman all noted that Granville Island's core brands seek to reach a wide range of beer drinkers. Goetz remarked, "We are more something for the broader population to appreciate. We offer a variety of flavour choices, but we don't push." Cosman added, "We are the safe choice of the craft-brew segment. Our customers have trust in our products." Lambourne commented, "We are authentic to the styles we brew; we don't want to go to extremes and frighten people. We want newcomers to craft beers to be comfortable."

This responsiveness to customers' tastes is reflected in early changes made to Granville Island Lager, the brewery's first, and still its best-selling, product. Goetz said, "It was initially fuller bodied and hoppier. We had to make it more conventional; it was too off-mainstream for many of them." It's a Bavarian-style lager, light-bodied and golden in colour, but with a maltier flavour than mainstream lagers.

English Bay Pale Ale, originally called Lord Stanley's Pale Ale, another early beer, was in the English style rather than the West Coast style popular in Washington State and Oregon. "The market here just wasn't ready for bitterness units above twenty," Goetz explained. "We made sure that the complex malt flavour balanced the hop bitterness." Gastown Amber, issued as Granville Island's tenth-anniversary ale is, Lambourne remarked, "a darker shade of pale. It takes a malt-based pale ale a step further. It's darker, fuller bodied, and more flavourful. But it's very smooth. It has sessionability."

Three beers are aimed directly at the crossover market. Robson Street Hefeweizen uses a traditional German yeast that gives banana and clove notes to this unfiltered beer. "We had to educate people about it at first," Cosman remembered, "but it has become a very popular summer drink." Cypress Honey Lager is a light-bodied, easy-drinking beer. In the brewing, Lambourne said, "We had to add just the right amount of honey to give the beer a smoothness, but not so much that it takes over the taste." The same is true of Kitsilano Maple Cream Ale. "The idea of adding maple

gave it a Canadian touch. It's close to a lager and it's very lightly hopped."

Two of Granville Island's recent additions to the core list move further away from the mainstream. Brockton IPA, which began as a special edition, was added to the regular list because, as Goetz remarked, "people are more adventurous now." Lambourne and Cosman has visited microbreweries in Seattle to discover what they were doing with their pale ales and decided that what they would offer as Granville Island's twenty-fifth-anniversary ale would be a West Coast-style India pale ale. "It's all about hops from the aroma to the finish," Lambourne said. At forty IBUs, it's double what the original pale ale was. However, the hop bitterness is not overwhelming, being balanced by the malty flavours. At 6 per cent ABV, it is the brewery's strongest offering. Lions Winter Ale, at 5.5 per cent, is not as strong, but it is darker, maltier, and fuller bodied than the other core beers. Its unique vanilla flavour profile is provided by white chocolate.

Lambourne spoke enthusiastically about the Limited Edition beers he creates on a regular basis. "It's not your average case of lout," he remarked, using the English term for inexpensive, mass-produced, inferior beer. Jolly Abbott is an abbey-style Belgian beer that checks in at 9 per cent ABV. Chocolate Stout uses chocolate from Victoria's well-known Rogers' Chocolates. The essential ingredient for Ginger Beer is purchased at the nearby Granville Island Public Market. "People are always asking us what's next and when. And they often want to know if we're going to bring back a favourite from a few years ago."

Molson Coors
   1550 Burrard St, Vancouver, V6J 3G5, 604-664-1786, molsoncoorscanada.com
Yaletown Brewing Company
   1111 Mainland St, Vancouver, V6B 5P2, 604-688-0084, markjamesgroup.com
Steamworks Brewing Company
   375 Water St, Vancouver, V6B 5C6, 604-689-2739, steamworks.com
Storm Brewing Limited
   310 Commercial Drive, Vancouver, V5L 3V6, 604-255-9119, stormbrewing.org
R&B Brewing Company
   54 East 4th Ave, Vancouver, V5T 1E8, 604-874-2537, r-and-b.com
Dockside Restaurant and Brewing Company
   1253 Johnston St, Vancouver, V6H 3R9, 604-685-7070, docksidebrewing.com
Granville Island Brewing Company
   1441 Cartwright St, Vancouver, V6H 3R7, 604-687-2739, gib.ca

CHAPTER EIGHT

Suds from Sea to Sky
North Vancouver to Whistler

Vancouver's Lions Gate Bridge marks the beginning of what is called the Sea to Sky Highway, the portion of Highway 99 that runs from North Vancouver to Whistler. It was along this road that John Mitchell and his partners opened North America's first brewpub, Horseshoe Bay Brewery and Troller Pub, in 1982. Today, there are two brewpub/microbreweries, a brewpub, and a microbrewery located between the north end of the bridge and downtown Whistler.

❖❖

North Vancouver's Taylor's Crossing Restaurant and Brewery, named in honour of Fred Taylor, the driving force behind the construction of the Lions Gate Bridge in the 1930s, stands two-and-a-half kilometres east of the bridge in a suburban shopping area. Opened in 2004, the most recent of the Mark James Group brewpubs, it has a restaurant, split-level bar area, summer patio, liquor store, and stand-alone brewery. Inside the brewpub are two fireplaces, a pool room, and a more than adequate number of large-screen televisions. Low-beamed ceilings and plank floors create the feeling of an English pub. Its standard pub fare menu is supplemented with Asian dishes. The brewery is home not only to the beers on the house menu, but also to Red Truck Ale and Lager, which are distributed on draft around Greater Vancouver.

Brewmaster Dave Varga became interested in the process of making beer when his microbiology professor at the University of British Columbia invited a few students to participate in a brewing "experiment" he was conducting in a corner of his lab. Before coming to the Mark James Group to open up Big Ridge in 1999, Varga learned his trade at a number of breweries. "At Whistler, I learned about brewing lagers; at Tree in Kelowna, about producing a range of styles; and at Brewsters in Calgary, about developing recipes—ones that you created and took responsibility for yourself."

Dave Varga is responsible for brewing not only the beers
served at Taylor's Crossing, but also Red Truck Ale and Lager,
which are available at Vancouver-area bars and restaurants.

He noted that, as was the case when Big Ridge opened, early customers at Taylor's Crossing were not highly knowledgeable about craft beers.
"I had to be more subdued to try to bring them in. I refined what people
were familiar with in order to coax them into new territory. I'm always

working to create better versions of accepted styles. I'm constantly tinkering with ingredients and processes."

The two Red Truck Beer products—which are named after "Old Weird Harry," the 1946 Dodge Power Wagon that used to deliver kegs—are entry-level or crossover beers. Red Truck Lager is a light gold, light-bodied, highly carbonated, all-malt beer with a clean finish. Red Truck Ale balances hops and malts. Lower in carbonation than the lager, it has caramel notes.

Two Lions Pale Ale, Indian Arm IPA, and Mad Scow Stout, brewed exclusively for Taylor's Crossing, take the brewpub's customers into more unfamiliar territory. Two Lions, an English pale ale that is very hoppy at forty IBUs, is golden-amber in colour and achieves a good balance of hops and malts. "Our English customers love it," Varga remarked. "Now that more people are accepting beers that are strongly hopped, we've added Indian Arm IPA. It uses American and English hops, but the malt profile prevents the hop bitterness, aroma, and flavour from becoming overwhelming." Mad Scow Stout is an Irish-style dry stout, "more like Beamish than Guinness, although the nitrogen infusion gives it the creamy body people associate with Guinness. There is a touch of sweetness and some hints of coffee." At 4 per cent ABV, it's designed to be a session beer.

Special releases allow Varga the opportunity to exercise his creativity. "I like to introduce people to styles they might not be familiar with, beers they wouldn't find in most liquor stores." These have included a German *roggen* (rye) beer, a Czech pilsner, an American steam beer, some Belgian ales, and a few English strong ales.

❖

For years, the town of Squamish, at the top of Howe Sound, was known as the southern terminus of the Pacific Great Eastern Railroad, the centre of the area's pulp-and paper-industry, and later as a pit stop on the way to Whistler. Gradually, it also became an appealing place to live. Away from the pressures of the Vancouver suburbs, it was cheaper than Whistler and had plenty of access to summer and winter recreation activities, including scaling Stawamus Chief, the world's second-largest granite rock face and a mecca for climbers from around the world. Its changed status was

Howe Sound's brewmaster, Franco Corno (left), and owner, Dave Fenn, display the brewery's unique one-litre, flip-top bottles. Begun as a brewpub, Howe Sound now distributes its bottled product throughout BC and Alberta, and in six American states.

reflected by the opening, in 1996, of **Howe Sound Inn and Brewing Company**, which has grown from a brewpub into a microbrewery that produces five thousand hectolitres annually and distributes in BC, Alberta, and six American states.

In the early 1990s, Squamish native Dave Fenn and his partner, Stephen Shard, with the assistance of microbrewing pioneer John Mitchell, examined the possibilities of opening a brewpub in the town. Early in the summer of 1996, Howe Sound Inn and Brewing Company—a brewpub, restaurant, and twenty-room hotel only a five-minute drive from the Sea to Sky highway and a two-minute walk from a local marina—opened. The restaurant and brewpub quickly became popular with summer and winter tourists but especially with the townspeople, who appreciated the hometown ownership, the local names given to several of the beers, and the establishment's involvement in community events.

After 2001, when provincial liquor regulations began allowing brew-pubs to sell their products off-premises, Howe Sound's business grew rapidly. For five years, their draft beer was sold in the Lower Mainland. Then in 2007, the company made the decision to package its beers in one-litre, flip-top (Grolsch-style) bottles. "At first, we used these bottles as a matter of expediency; they were easier to fill," Fenn explained. But he went on to say that because they were different in size and shape from other beer bottles in liquor stores, they were more easily noticed by poten-tial buyers. "The bottles also reflect our philosophy about drinking beer. We wanted to move beer off the couch to the dining table." The larger size meant that two or three people could share a bottle during dinner.

Getting known in the crowded BC microbrew market was difficult. "We used word of mouth, involved ourselves in community events, held tastings at bars and liquor stores, and attended beer festivals," Fenn noted. Giving two of their products clever names garnered attention. "During the financial crisis in 2008, we brainstormed about how to give a little humour to a grim situation. We came up with the idea of brewing an ordinary bitter and calling it 'Bailout Bitter.' We had a label showing a graph indicating the downward financial trend. The local media ran a story and it was picked up all around the world."

They also wanted to do something related to the 2010 Winter Olympics, but, like R&B in Vancouver, they faced a challenge because of the strict regulations regarding the use of terms relating to the Games. They came up with something that was funny, Canadian, and about win-ning medals. They created a robust (7 per cent ABV) amber ale, named it

Three Beavers Ale, and designed a label that showed three of the toothy animals, each wearing a medal—one gold, one silver, and one bronze. They were on safe grounds legally because the medals on the label were those that Howe Sound had won in international brewing competitions. Global Language Monitor, a Texas research company, declared it the most effective marketing campaign relating to the 2010 Games.

Howe Sound's ales reflect the English heritage of John Mitchell, who developed the recipes and acted as brewer during the first few years. Current brewmaster Franco Corno, who learned to brew under the guidance of Frank Appleton, Mitchell's consultant for the setting up of Horseshoe Bay Brewery, noted that six of the eight year-round beers, and six of the seven seasonal or limited edition beers, are based on English styles.

The core list of beers ranges from mild, at thirteen IBUs, to very hoppy, at sixty-eight. Whitecap Wheat Ale, the only non-English style on the regular list, is a Belgian *wit*, which, at thirteen IBUs and 4.5 per cent ABV, is the least assertive of the beers. Light- to medium-bodied and highly carbonated, it is flavoured with orange peel and coriander. Garibaldi Honey Pale Ale and Diamond Head Oatmeal Stout are only slightly more hopped, and each is rated at sixteen IBUs. Both are 5 per cent ABV. In the former, which has BC honey added in the boil, malty notes dominate. Effervescent and clean-finishing, it is designed as a session beer. The stout has coffee and chocolate notes, is medium- to full-bodied, and has a sweet, creamy finish.

Rail Ale started out as a stout before being changed into an English brown. Nine malts give it coffee and chocolate notes. Full-bodied and smooth, it is the top-selling Howe Sound product. Baldwin and Cooper Best Bitter, named after the first two people to climb the Chief—as locals fondly call the rock face—is a classic extra special bitter. "English customers love it; they say it reminds them of home," Corno noted. Light gold in colour, it has a crisp mouth-feel. The hop bitterness, a fairly strong fifty-two IBUs, is moderated by the malty flavours. Devil's Elbow India Pale Ale has, according to the advertising copy, "a well-deserved following among hop lovers." It has been described as starting with a hop rush which, because of malty notes, is neither abrasive nor overwhelming. It is rated at sixty-eight IBUs.

The brewery's seasonal-release list is dominated by Imperial beers, which traditionally means those with a higher alcohol content, usually at least 7 per cent ABV. In addition to the Three Beavers Amber, there are four members of the John Mitchell Special Series, each designed to honour the pioneer brewer. Father John's Winter Ale is a malty, 7 per cent ABV beer, with ginger notes. Pumpkin Eater Imperial Ale, which adds roasted pumpkin to the mash and is spiced with anise, cinnamon, and nutmeg, and Total Eclipse of the Hop IPA, a ninety IBU brew that uses six hop varieties, are each 8 per cent ABV. Pothole Filler Russian Imperial Stout, described as "thick enough to fill potholes," tops the list at 9 per cent ABV.

The BrewHouse at Whistler, which opened in 1997, the second of the Mark James Group brewpubs, shares many characteristics with the other three. It has a bar, restaurant, and patio, several television sets, and a pool table. It serves Red Truck Ale, and the menu includes ribs, wings, Caesar salad, pizza, and burgers. But, as is the case with the other three, it has its own character, shaped by its location and clientele and its brewer. In the centre of one of the world's most famous winter resort towns, it is surrounded by high-end restaurants, clothing stores, and sporting goods shops.

Expensive hotels and condominiums are a short distance away. To the east and south are the snow slopes seen by the millions of people who watched the 2010 Winter Olympics on television. Most of the people who stroll the streets are not local; they're well-heeled tourists from Vancouver, the American Pacific Northwest, and the wide world beyond. Often they leave their skis at the door of the brewhouse. They are different from the business people and after-hockey and after-football crowds that visit Yaletown, and the suburbanites who frequent Taylor's Crossing and Big Ridge. Fresh from the outdoors, guests bring healthy appetites with them. And, because most walk back to their hotels and condos from the restaurant, they may enjoy more than one beer.

Dave Woodward, who has been brewing for these customers since 2005, was learning to become a stonemason in his hometown of Qualicum Beach on Vancouver Island when his part-time job working

Dave Woodward has cramped quarters in which to work because,
when the BrewHouse at Whistler was being built, the designer
put enough space for two pool tables in an adjacent room.

at a brew-on-premises convinced him that "making beer was more
interesting than breaking stone." He earned a diploma in brewing at the
University of Sunderland and apprenticed for two years at a microbrewery in England before returning to BC, where he got to know Yaletown's

brewmaster Iain Hill. When the job in Whistler opened up, Hill recommended him for it.

"Because Lifty Lager is our best seller, one of my first jobs when I got here was to learn about lagers. After that, I was pretty much left to develop beers that reflected my interests. Now, I brew the beers I like for people who love beer. The creativity comes from understanding both the ingredients and process, and then tinkering with them. Because of my interest in the English tradition, I like session beers, which is good for our customers. They're often tourists who don't like their beers to be too extreme."

Lifty Lager (named after the people who operate the ski lifts) is German-style beer. Crisp, clear, and golden, it uses Munich malts to give it more body than mainstream beers and to impart a toasty flavour. "The soft Whistler water is great for lagers," Woodward noted. "In fact, when I'm making ales, I have to make the water harder." The English Fuggle hops impart earthy notes. "Because of my English training, it's a little darker and hoppier than German lagers."

Red Truck Ale, which is basically the same as the Red Truck found at the other Mark James brewpubs, and Grizzly Brown Ale move into the darker and more full-bodied range. Both are 5 per cent ABV in comparison to the lager's 4.5 per cent. The brown ale is in the northern English style, which is not as sweet as the well-known Newcastle Brown, and is also roastier than many examples of the style. It is characterized by a rich maltiness and, because it is nitrogen-infused, it has a creamy, smooth mouth-feel.

Big Wolf Bitter and Woodward's IPA lead the BrewHouse's guests into more adventurous beer-drinking territory. Although at 5.4 per cent ABV the bitter is higher in alcohol than most examples of the popular English session beer, it is not, at thirty IBUs, too bitter. "English people don't want their bitters to blow them away; the Fuggle hops we use provide earthy notes, and the English malts add a biscuit flavour." True to the style, it is low in carbonation and is not served chilled. Woodward's IPA, at 6.7 per cent ABV, is the strongest beer on the core list, and is, the brewmaster admits, "my favourite." Inspired to create it while attending a craft brewers' conference in San Diego, Woodward visited breweries in Oregon and Washington to learn more about this West Coast style.

Crisp, with a clean, dry finish, it uses Northwest varieties of hops to produce grapefruit and tangerine notes. "It has character, but it's not overwhelming. My dad was very proud that I gave it the family name."

Like most microbrewers, Dave exhibits his creative and adventurous side in his special edition beers. These have included a raspberry wheat ale with a noticeable pink tinge, which he introduced during a Gay Pride Week celebration in Whistler; Heart of Darkness Imperial Stout, an 8 per cent ABV beverage that is aged in oak barrels that once stored bourbon; and the 8.5 per cent ABV Dave's Dam Dangerously Drinkable Double IPA.

❖❖

On December 2, 2009, **Whistler Brewing Company** ended its nearly nine-year exile from the mountain resort town. The exile had begun in the spring of 2001, when Big Rock Brewery of Calgary purchased the Whistler and Bowen Island brands and began brewing them in Kamloops. The acquisition was not designed to add popular BC brands to Big Rock's portfolio, but to provide the Alberta company with an opportunity to begin brewing its own products in BC. The two brands were allowed to decline.

In 2003, Bruce Dean, a one-time executive with Gillette, whom Big Rock had hired to evaluate their BC operations, recommended that they concentrate on their BC brands, particularly Whistler Brewing. "By that time, the town of Whistler had been awarded the 2010 Olympic Games. Whistler itself was known around the world for its mountains, forests, clear lakes and streams, and for its hiking, golfing, mountain biking, and skiing. BC drinkers were very enthusiastic about craft beers and the Whistler and Bowen Island brands had built up loyal followings during the 1990s."

When Big Rock executives declined to follow his advice, Dean gathered a group of investors and purchased Whistler Brewing in the fall of 2005. "We acquired the Kamloops brewery and some kegs, the proprietary rights to the Bear, Bowen Island, and Whistler beers, and the contracts to brew for Earls and Joey Tomato's restaurants." At the time, only one Whistler beer, Premium Export Lager, was produced, and it was available only on draft.

In 2005, when Bruce Dean put together a group of investors to purchase Whistler Brewing, the brand was languishing. The company, which brews in both Kamloops and Whistler, has since become one of BC's largest microbreweries.

Then the hard work began. The new owners developed five styles of beer that would be available year-round. They created custom bottles and expensive foil labels, decorated with a commissioned painting of Whistler. "It's the most premium packaging in western Canada," Dean noted proudly. Perhaps most important, the brewery started shipping water from Whistler to Kamloops. Every week or two, a truck carrying four hundred hectolitres of what brewers call "liquid" would arrive at the Kamloops plant. The importation of the water wasn't just a matter of making sure that the Kamloops-brewed product had a direct connection with Whistler; it was also because the mountain water was excellent for making the company's lagers.

"We had good beer, good packaging, and a great name," Dean remarked. "I hoped that Whistler beer would become associated with vacations to BC in the same way that Corona was associated with trips to Mexican resorts." He expanded the beer's distribution to Alberta, to the northwest states of Montana, Washington, Idaho, and Oregon, and abroad to Japan, China, and Australia (Dean's native country). "If people from those places purchase some Whistler beer, I hope they'll remember their visit to Whistler or, if they haven't been here, they'll think about coming."

Under Dean's guidance, Kamloops Brewery, as it was renamed after the takeover, grew quickly; sales and production capacity increased tenfold. By 2010, fifty employees worked at the Kamloops plant, which is now called Northam Brewery, producing, selling, and distributing over forty thousand hectolitres of beer annually. But, except for the name, the picture on the bottle, and the water content of the product inside, Whistler beer was Whistler in name only.

That changed in December 2009, just over two months before the Olympics began, when Whistler Brewing opened a small brewery in the old Whistler Transit maintenance facility, a ten-minute drive from the centre of town. "We think it was good business for us and for the community. Now we're part of the community, hiring local people. And we're close to our water supply." The twenty-hectolitre facility is the ideal size for running test brews and making limited edition and seasonal beers. It's also designed to take some of the pressure off the increasingly busy Kamloops plant by producing draft to serve the Whistler Corridor, from Squamish to Pemberton, and packaging canned versions of the brewery's pale ale and lager.

Premium Export Lager, one of the original brews, is the best-selling of Whistler's year-round beers. Golden and light-bodied, this highly carbonated beer strikes a balance between hops and malts, neither of which is strongly pronounced. Altitude Honey Lager, amber in colour,

is a smooth, medium-bodied beer in which the noticeable honey flavour does not overwhelm. There is a slight hop finish. Weissbier, available only in the warmer months, is an unfiltered German *hefeweizen*, featuring notes of clove, banana, and citrus. Medium-bodied and smooth, it has won gold medals in both the Canadian Brewing and the North American Brewing awards competitions.

Classic Pale Ale is an amber, lightly hopped, English-style beer. Smooth and effervescent, it has caramel malt flavours. Black Tusk Ale is an English dark mild, deep brown and almost opaque. It has coffee and chocolate notes, and almost no evidence of hops. Smooth, rich, and mildly carbonated, it is very close to being a stout.

Taylor's Crossing Restaurant and Brewery
　　1035 Marine Dr, North Vancouver, V7P 1S6, 604-986-7899, markjamesgroup.com
Howe Sound Inn and Brewing Company
　　37801 Cleveland Ave, Squamish, V8B 0A7, 604-892-2603, howesound.com
BrewHouse at Whistler
　　4355 Blackcomb Way, Whistler, V0N 1B4, 604-905-2739, markjamesgroup.com
Whistler Brewing Company
　　1045 Miller Creek Rd, Whistler, V0N 1B1, 604-962-8889, whistlerbeer.com

ANCOUVER
AND STYLE

HER

Vancouver Island

Part Four

Vancouver Island

In 1860, when mainland British Columbia's first brewery opened in New Westminster, Victoria's first brewery had been operating for two years. William Steinberger had started a small brewery near Swan Lake in 1858 and moved it a year later to the corner of Government and Discovery in downtown Victoria, where it operated as Victoria Brewery. Five years later, Mill Street Brewery opened in Nanaimo. Between the two cities, over a dozen breweries operated before the twentieth century, another briefly did business in Cumberland.

Many of these breweries were short-lived, frequently undergoing name changes and transfers of ownership but there were two exceptions. In 1880, Nanaimo Brewery opened on the site of the Mill Street plant and, in 1890, it merged with a newly formed brewery to become Union Brewery. It went out of business in 1918, a victim of Prohibition. In Victoria, descendants of William Steinberger's brewery operated until 1981. In 1893, Victoria Brewery merged with Phoenix Brewing (founded in 1864) and then, in 1928, the company became part of the Coast Breweries consortium. In 1954, it was renamed Lucky Lager Brewery, which was bought by Labatt in 1958—one of a number of purchases the Ontario brewery made in its move to become national. Labatt closed the plant in 1981 and shortly afterwards demolished it.

Within two years, the microbrewing movement arrived on the island. In 1983, Prairie Inn Pub and Cottage Brewery opened in Saanichton, just north of Victoria. A year later, Spinnakers became Canada's first in-house brewpub. Island Pacific Brewing Company began operations in Saanichton in 1985, and North Island Brewing of Campbell River opened in 1986. Of these pioneer breweries, only Spinnakers and Island Pacific (now Vancouver Island Brewery) still exist.

LONGWOOD
BREWERY

THE SPIRIT OF THE ISLAND

CHAPTER NINE

Island Hopping
Campbell River to Salt Spring Island

"Go North. Get Lucky!"

This command is not an expression of a teen-aged boy's dreams; it's a cynical statement made by many microbrewers to describe the dominant beer culture on Vancouver Island. "Lucky" is a reference to Lucky Lager beer, which was brewed in Victoria until 1982, then in New Westminster, and, since 2005, in Creston, British Columbia. Since 1958, it has been the top-selling value-priced beer in Labatt's portfolio. The idea behind the saying is that the farther north people travel from Victoria, the more drinkers of Lucky Lager they will find. Because of the amount of the beer consumed, the Cowichan Valley, near Duncan, has been called "The Valley of Lucky Lager" and Cumberland, north of Nanaimo, "The Luckiest Town in Canada."

However, in spite of the brand's overwhelming popularity, there are three microbreweries and three brewpubs north of Victoria. Two of them are north of Nanaimo in an area about which craft brewers have said, "Every mile you go north of Nanaimo it becomes harder and harder to sell your beer."

❖

Merecroft Village Pub, the island's longest-running brewpub north of Victoria, is in Campbell River, what some would call the "heart" of Lucky country. MVP, as it is called by locals, began business in 1996 as Cogg 'n' Kettle, when the owners of Vancouver's Steamworks decided to take advantage of the area's burgeoning tourist industry. MVP is divided into a bar area and restaurant. The bar has a pool table, plenty of television sets, and a feature reminiscent of Steamworks: the mash tun, brew kettle, and three fermenters on display along the back wall.

Three beers are brewed on site, down from six a decade ago. Harley Smith, head brewer at Nanaimo's Longwood Brewpub, comes up to Campbell River on his days off to brew what's needed. "I do beers for

Merecroft Village Pub, in a Campbell River shopping centre, is the longest-operating Vancouver Island brewpub north of Victoria.

that market," he explained as he began to describe the three. Maple Leaf Logger, he called "maple more in name than beer." It's a dark gold, smooth, North American lager, with virtually no taste of hops and just a hint of maple syrup. The Village Nut, an English brown ale which has, Smith said, "been lightened," is mildly malty with a smooth mouth-feel. Railway India Pale Ale is an understated beer with just a little more trace of hops than the lager has of maple syrup. These are gentle crossover beers, not at all threatening to Lucky drinkers. Along with the taps for the pub's own beers are six others dispensing Molson, Labatt, and Sleeman products. For those who choose none of these, a beer cooler is filled with bottles of imports and cans of a variety of domestic brews—including Lucky.

Comox's Surgenor Brewing Company was formed because Bob Surgenor decided to provide work for the people in his electrical contracting company during an economic slowdown, to turn his homebrewing hobby

Owner Bob Surgenor (left) and brewmaster Martin Eschbaumer
stand beside the new equipment at Surgenor Brewing of Comox.

into a profession, and to offer Lucky Lager drinkers something different—but not too different. In the spring of 2009, after three years of
raising capital, consulting with people in the beer business, meeting with
liquor officials and local zoning boards, and building his brewery (called
The Red House because of the colour of its siding), he began to brew
and sell beer, first on draft and then in aluminum bottles.

He decided on aluminum bottles because "they're lightweight, easy
to transport and to recycle, almost unbreakable—and they cool the
beer quickly." Moreover, because they were different, they stood out on
liquor store shelves. However, after a year, Surgenor decided to change to
brown glass bottles. "You had to order such a huge quantity of labelled
aluminum bottles for each style of beer that it limited your flexibility.
With glass bottles, we can offer a variety of styles, and all we have to do
is put different labels on the bottles."

Outside of Comox, where as a local boy with plenty of contacts he
found people receptive to his beers, he discovered that breaking into
the beer market was a challenge. "The resistance has gradually gone

from being very heavy to mild. We had to be persistent, to give tastings, to attend area events. Port Alberni and Campbell River were tough to crack. But north of that, in Port Hardy, Port McNeill, and Port Alice, people really liked our beers." After a year, his product became available throughout Vancouver Island and in the Lower Mainland. Annual production is now over three thousand hectolitres.

Surgenor Brewing offers four products: Red House Ale, Steam Donkey Lager, In Seine Pale Ale, and #8 Shaft Black Lager. The first is named after the brewery itself, the other three pay tribute to the area's logging, fishing, and mining industries, respectively. "We designed our recipes knowing that this was lager country," Surgenor said, referring to the first two products brewed, Red House Ale and Steam Donkey Lager. "Both of them are accessible, but they have a depth of flavour and a pronounced hop bitterness that distinguishes them from most North American lagers." Steam Donkey is a Czech-style pilsner, golden in colour with a degree of malty sweetness but a crisp hop finish. Red House Ale, which he called an Irish red ale, is darker and fuller bodied than the lager.

After he made the decision to use glass bottles, Surgenor expanded the number of styles he offered. Munich-trained brewmaster Martin Eschbaumer developed In Seine Pale Ale to be smoother and a little closer than most pale ales to what mainstream drinkers were familiar with. Although it is a West Coast-style pale ale, it does not have the strong bitterness of the style. "I've added a little wheat to give a fuller flavour that balances the hops." The Northwest hops he used also provide a fruity aroma. #8 Shaft Black Lager is a *Schwarzbier*, a style Eschbaumer got plenty of experience brewing back in Germany. "It has a strong malty taste, but it is relatively light-bodied, and it has a refreshing, clean finish."

Surgenor Brewing is making gradual inroads into what has been the entrenched North American-lager culture north of Nanaimo. "We've given blind taste tests to people who say that they wouldn't drink anything but Lucky Lager," Eschbaumer recalled. "And most of them say they like our beers better. It's a matter of educating the beer drinkers around here."

Before Bunny Goodman (left) and Rob Haseloh decided to begin
Fat Cat Brewery, the latter worked as a motorcycle mechanic.

For the three-quarters of a century after Empire Brewing closed in
1921, residents of Nanaimo—which in the 1950s was reputed to have
more beer parlours per capita than any other Canadian city—had to
depend on breweries in Victoria and the Lower Mainland for their suds.
Then, in 1997, Bastion City Brewing opened in Cassidy, just south of
Nanaimo. Within a few months though, the owners found themselves
with no liquid assets (literal and metaphorical). After Bastion folded,
homebrewers Rob Haseloh, a motorcycle mechanic, and Bunny
Goodman, a print shop supervisor, decided to start **Fat Cat Brewery**.

The difficulties the couple had in starting their brewery and then
keeping it going sound like a brewer's version of the Book of Job. After
they had purchased Bastion City's equipment, they found that they
would have to dismantle it and move it to storage facilities. On July 1,
1999, when they arrived at the new building where they had leased space
for the brewery, they discovered that the walls separating their space from
other businesses had not been built and that the concrete floor had been
poured in such a way that water and spilt beer could not easily flow into

the drains. After the walls were up, they began to construct the brewery themselves, working before and after their day jobs.

In addition to co-ordinating the visits of a number of city inspectors, no easy task, Goodman had to battle the hydro company, which insisted that the power had been hooked up. It had—to another building. Then the person sent to hook up the gas arrived several days after his scheduled appointment, looked at the facility, and announced he didn't have the appropriate certification to do the job. On the first day of brewing, work came to an abrupt standstill as police cars screeched into the parking lot and officers converged on the unit next door. Their neighbours were operating a sizeable grow-op, making good money from a plant related to hops.

Finally, in January 2000, the brewery opened for business. It was named Fat Cat, Goodman said, because research showed that mono-syllabic rhyming names are easily recognizable. "I remembered that the politician Pat Carney had talked about the 'Fat Cats' out on the West Coast, and we were anything but fat cats. So the name was partly tongue in cheek." They marketed two products: Fat Head India Pale Ale (named after a man Goodman had once worked for) and Fat Cat Pilsner. Marketed on draft around the Nanaimo area, the two brews met with limited success. "We had to tone the IPA down," Haseloh said. "People thought it was too bitter. And after a couple of years, we dropped the pilsner because people found it too flavourful."

Problems developed when Fat Cat decided to open a retail outlet at the brewery. Goodman advertised that the store would open in mid-June of 2001 but the Liquor Distribution Branch informed them that there had been a mix-up with their licence. By the time things were straightened out, it was the middle of August, and Fat Cat had lost nearly two months of the best sales period of the year.

Another difficulty arose when Fat Cat decided to distribute in 650-millilitre bottles. "We ordered a bottling machine from California and it didn't arrive. After five months, we headed to the States and discovered it lying in pieces on the factory floor. The people had spent our money but done nothing for us. And now they didn't have any money to give us a refund. We camped out at their factory until they did the job and then we brought the machine home."

With beer in bottles, Goodman and Haseloh could distribute their

product to government and private liquor stores on the island and in the Lower Mainland. "We don't go beyond Qualicum Beach [a resort area north of Nanaimo]," Haseloh remarked, a smile on his face. "You know what they say—the farther north you go, the Luckier you get. There just isn't the market for our kinds of beer up there."

Fat Cat's annual production is modest—just over five hundred and fifty hectolitres—but size has never been a concern for Goodman and Haseloh. "Quality is the most important thing for us. None of our product leaves here spoiled. If it doesn't pass over our tongues, it doesn't go out, and we'll yank it off the shelves if it's stale. Sometimes you only get one chance at a customer. Quality—it's all we have."

The brewery produces four year-round beers and one seasonal. "Our beers are for people with educated palates, people who've found they can enjoy good beer and not have a hangover." The 6 per cent ABV India Pale Ale, which has been available in six-packs of 341-millilitre bottles since the late spring of 2010, is the top seller. "When we reduced its hoppiness," Haseloh commented, "it became more of an English-style IPA, with a good balance between hops and malts." Low in carbonation, it is golden-amber in colour.

The number two seller, Honey Beer, was developed after the two decided to drop their pilsner. "First, we developed a cream ale, which was close to an English-style pale ale. But when it didn't go over, we used it as the base for our honey ale. We use Honeydew Honey from New Zealand. It's collected from the sap of the beech tree and has the consistency of maple syrup." The hint of honey imparts a malty flavour to the beer, which is smooth, effervescent, and clean finishing.

About Pompous Pompadour Porter, which the advertising copy calls "a big name for a big beer," Haseloh noted wryly, "It's the most awesome product you'll ever get. Everyone should have one for breakfast." It's an opaque brown colour and pours with a rich brown head. The malts provide chocolatey notes. The porter also serves as one of the ingredients for Goodman's Black and Tan. The other is the India Pale Ale. "It looks dark, but it isn't heavy," said Goodman, who suggested the combination. "The mixture of the more bitter pale ale and the malty porter makes just the right mix. I love having a glass of it while I'm watching Sunday-morning reruns of *Coronation Street*." Haseloh also produces an annual batch of Old Bad Cat Barley Wine, an 11.5 per cent ABV ale that is cask-conditioned in bourbon barrels.

In December 2010, the brewery was sold and renamed Wolf Brewing Company. The new owners planned to use Hasleoh's recipes.

❖

When visitors enter **Longwood Brewpub**, located in an upscale shopping centre ten minutes north of downtown Nanaimo, it quickly becomes evident that this isn't one of your old-style Nanaimo beer parlours. Just inside the front entrance, behind floor-to-ceiling glass walls, stands a modern, stainless steel, ten-hectolitre brewing system. On the main floor, cherrywood walls, jatoba flooring (made from Brazilian cherrywood), and a wood-burning fireplace give the large restaurant an air of elegance. Downstairs, cosy booths, another fireplace, a pool table, and a dart board evoke the atmosphere of an English pub. There are a couple of television sets, but as Barry Ladell, one of the original owners and now the publican, noted, "We're not a sports bar; people come here to talk to each other."

Ladell, who had been a homebrewer and a maître d' in fine restaurants in Victoria, became a fan of Spinnakers when it opened in 1984, discovering, he said, how good real ales were. One day, he walked into the Victoria brewpub and offered to manage the restaurant if John Mitchell would teach him how to brew on a commercial scale. By the early 1990s, Ladell had risen to the position of head brewer at Spinnakers, a job he held for a few years before beginning his own consulting company, helping people set up and operate brewpubs. Among his clientele was a group that was planning to open a brewpub in Nanaimo. "I looked at the Longwood area and realized that this would be an ideal location; it was growing and the new residents had disposable income." He designed the restaurant and brewpub, developed recipes for several beers, and trained staff.

"Real ale has to go with real food," Ladell remarked, noting that without good beer, the establishment couldn't have become the success it has. "Beer is the centre of it all." For nearly a decade, the making of that beer has been the responsibility of Harley Smith, who came to Nanaimo after working at brewpubs and a microbrewery in Ontario and for Steamworks brewpub in Vancouver. He spoke of his preference for working at brewpubs rather than microbreweries. "At brewpubs, you

LONGWOOD

VANCOUVER ISLAND STYLE

LONGWOOD ALE

Handcrafted

BREWERY

ER

...od & Bottled by Longwood Brew Pub, Nana...

Barry Ladell, one of the original owners and now the publican at Nanaimo's Longwood Brewpub, is one of several former employees of Victoria's Spinnakers Gastro Brewpub who have gone on to distinguished careers in the microbrewing or brewpub business.

don't get stuck in one area; here, you do everything from ordering ingredients, to making beer, packaging it, and selling it. You can make such a wonderful variety of beers. You create your own recipes and then see the customers appreciate what you've created. Consistency isn't the main object, like it is in microbreweries. You're always tweaking your recipes."

Asked to describe the general character of Longwood's beers, Ladell referred to the Two Bs—basic and balanced. "I'm a style person, and I like our beers to reflect the basic qualities of the styles. I also like balanced beers, ones in which the hops and malts complement each other. We're not big on aggressive beers; we don't go to extremes." Smith added, "If you know the history of beer styles, you won't be surprised when you try ours." Of the seven core beers, only the Czech pilsner and the Dunkel Weizen are not English styles. Three of the beers are drawn with traditional beer engines, hand pumps that bring the beverage to the taps without using pressurized carbon dioxide.

The two lightest beers on the list are Longwood Ale and Lulu's Lager. The former is a smooth, light- to medium-bodied blonde ale that emphasizes malty flavours over a moderate bitterness. "It's our crossover beer for craft-beer beginners and it makes a very good session beer," Smith said. Lulu's Lager, named for a nearby performing-arts camp, uses Saaz hops to create a light, crisp mouth-feel and a moderate bitterness, and to contribute aromas and flavours. The Dunkel Weizen is, as its German name suggests, an oxymoron, a dark-coloured, unfiltered German wheat beer that uses chocolate and black malts for flavour and colouring. The Canadian wheat malt, which accounts for 35 per cent of the malt used, provides a light body and a clean, crisp mouth-feel.

The India Pale Ale is an English rather than West Coast style. It's strong—6.8 per cent ABV—and bitter—fifty-five IBUs. "It's like the kind people drank in England in the middle of the nineteenth century," Smith explained. "We use English hops: Fuggles to impart earthy notes and East Kent to give a fruity aroma. The English malts give body to support and balance the generous amount of hops." Light amber in colour, the ale has a crisp hop finish.

The Extra Special Bitter is based on the classic English style developed by John Mitchell at Troller and Spinnakers. Contrary to its name, it is a smooth, mild beer. "It's very popular with our British expats," Ladell noted. The Irish Red, which is like an Irish cream ale, has sweetness imparted by caramel malts and virtually no hop presence. "Irish Reds are a lot about the smoothness and the thick creamy heads," Smith said. Russian Imperial Stout, a style of beer the English exported to the czar, is, in Smith's words, "the granddaddy of stout." He calls it a big beer,

Liz Steward, co-owner of Duncan's Craig Street Brew Pub, and brewer
Chris Gress offer area beer drinkers a number of alternatives to Lucky Lager.

rich and chewy. Even though it is 7.5 per cent ABV, it is an extremely
flavourful beer, with hops and malts complementing each other.

For those who have not been won over by Smith's creations, Kokanee
and Coors Light are also available at the brewpub. That's all. "A fellow
came up to the bar and asked me what I had that tasted like Lucky,"
Smith remembered, laughing. "I told him, 'Nothing, I hope.'"

❖

In 2006, when Craig Street Brew Pub opened in the middle of downtown Duncan, a small city sixty-five kilometres north of Victoria, many
people wondered why anyone would decide to open a brewpub at the
eastern entrance to the Cowichan Valley, "The Valley of Lucky Lager."
But the decision wasn't a whim on the part of the owners, Liz and Lance
Steward. The pair had operated Just Jakes, a respected Duncan restaurant, for nearly fifteen years. Great fans of Spinnakers, Canoe, and Swans
in Victoria, they knew that the Duncan liquor store ranked in the top
25 per cent in the province for sales of imported beers. They felt that the
area was ready for this kind of restaurant and bar—and, as Liz remarked,

"We wanted to give Lucky drinkers the taste of something different. When we were designing the facility, we stole ideas from Swans and Spinnakers in Victoria, and Yaletown in Vancouver."

The brewpub is a four-level affair. The brewery, bar, and restaurant are on the ground floor; a mezzanine level has a small, snug-like pub area; on the third floor is the library—not really a library, although there are low bookshelves along the walls. Here are Craig Street's only two television sets, and the library is crowded on Vancouver Canucks's game nights, as it is when local musicians are invited to perform. During the summer, the fourth level, a rooftop deck and barbecue area, is open.

On a pillar near the entrance, a framed plaque states the credo of Chris Gress, Craig Street's first and only brewmaster: "When I grew up in Northern Saskatchewan, my grandfather told me that if I could find a job I truly enjoy, one: I would be a lucky man, and two: the job wouldn't feel like work. He was right. I don't just enjoy my job, I love it."

Gress became interested in microbreweries when he moved to Victoria in the early 1990s. He met Swans' first brewmaster, Sean Hoyne, and then built a pilot brewery in his own backyard, where he brewed for his Camosun College friends, the Brew Engineers as they called themselves, and listened to their feedback. While he was working at a Victoria bar, he kidded a group of people from Duncan that "there was no good beer in Duncan" and learned from them about plans for Craig Street. He applied for the brewer's job, got it, and, with the help of Hoyne, designed and set up the brewing equipment and began considering what beers to create.

"I noticed that in Duncan it seemed people were drinking either Lucky or imports," Gress remembered. "So I visualized a colour spectrum of beers from light to dark. I decided to be right down the middle in my interpretation of styles. I could push the envelope and be as creative as I wanted when I brewed limited edition seasonal beers. At first, I was pretty traditional. Now I'm more creative. I blend my yeasts and experiment with hops. But this isn't a hop-based beer culture, so I have to go easy."

Cowichan Bay Lager, the first beer Gress brewed and, not surprisingly given the area, the brewpub's best seller, was designed to lure Lucky drinkers. Light-bodied, this light gold, German-style beer is crisp and clean. Very light on hops, it has a hint of malt sweetness. Arbutus Pale Ale, his second creation, is also light-bodied and gold in colour. An English-style beer, it's only mildly hoppy and achieves a balance between hops and malts. "It's only thirty IBUs, not a high number even for a pale ale," Gress commented, "but it's our way of introducing hopped beers to the people of this area."

Shawnigan Irish Red, the brewpub's second-best-selling beer, features what Gress refers to as "heavier, bolder malting. It's what you might call a beery beer, but it doesn't seem heavy because of the natural carbonation." Mt. Prevost Porter, is "such a neat beer," Gress enthused. "It's great in beer culture markets, but harder to sell here. So I was really surprised when I took it off our list a couple of years ago and people asked me to put it back." Dark in colour and medium-bodied, it has coffee notes and a dry finish.

Many of the seasonal beers Gress has brewed depart from the familiar "down the middle" characteristic of the four core beers. They also depart from the naming of each beer for a nearby locale. Among the more interesting are Asp Kisser Egyptian Hibiscus Ale, McGillivarian Bavarian Marzen, and Skinny Lizard Brown Ale. And, oh yes, they do serve Lucky Lager. "It's our biggest seller in bottles," Liz Steward reported. In the summer of 2010, Craig Street announced expansion plans that included the installation of bottling facilities. The brewpub's beers will take their place in local liquor stores, not far from bottles of Lucky.

❖❖

In the mid-1990s, Murray Hunter, the owner of a Salt Spring Island brew-on-premises, decided to sponsor a bus trip for his customers to Victoria's Great Canadian Beer Festival. It was on the way home that he and Bob Ellison discussed the idea of opening a microbrewery on Salt Spring Island. The local school board had plans for a one-hundred-and-eighty-five-square-metre barn, and sold them a copy for five dollars. The two then built **Gulf Islands Brewing's** brewery at the foot of Mount Bruce. It is set in a grove of cedars, some of which provided the building's siding. They sold their first batch of beer in September 1998.

Why, Hunter has often been asked, did he and Ellison decide to start a brewery on an island where the population was not much more than

Located on Salt Spring Island, Gulf Islands Brewing distributes
a great deal of its product in Victoria. Co-founder and brewer
Murray Hunter makes a delivery of freshly brewed beer.

ten thousand and from which they'd have to take a ferry to bring their
product to the craft-beer-savvy Greater Victoria market? "We felt there
was a sufficient base of people with educated beer palates here—people
who drank beer to enjoy the flavour, not the alcohol," Hunter remarked.
"The other 80 per cent would never stop drinking Lucky. We also wanted
to give something back to the island, to buy local products and to create
a beer that reflected the lifestyle of people here, somewhat laid back, not
too assertive. And there's a spring on Bob's farm, where the brewery is,
that's pure and clean and ideal for brewing beer." In 2010, a local farmer
began to supply the brewery with hops, and there was talk of planting
barley in the area.

"We are truly a cottage brewery," Hunter emphasized, drawing parallels between Gulf Islands Brewing and Crannog Ales, in the interior of
the province. "They're small, they're out in the country on a farm, they
use water from the farm, and they buy local materials. We've bought
some of their organic hops from them." Like Crannog, Gulf Islands
brews just over six hundred hectolitres of beer a year.

The brewery's first beer, and still its top seller, is Salt Spring Golden Ale,
the winner of two Canadian Brewing Awards gold medals. Unfiltered, it

has grapefruit notes balanced by a nutty malt flavour. Hunter described it as "light-bodied and light-coloured, like Molson Canadian, but with a lot more flavour. It's our session beer." At twenty IBUs, the hops provide some bitterness and contribute to a crisp, clean finish.

Salt Spring Golden Ale is available on draft and in 650-millilitre bottles, as are Salt Spring Pale Ale and Salt Spring Porter. Originally brewed for a popular restaurant near the Victoria International Airport, the pale ale is described as a cross between two famous English beers, Marston's Burton Bitter and Samuel Smith's Pale Ale. The English hops and roasted barley create a balance of flavours—toasty caramel notes along with spiciness and a crisp hop finish. A deep copper colour, it's darker than most pale ales. Salt Spring Porter is relatively light bodied for the style. Chocolate and toffee flavours dominate, but Cascade hops provide a fruity aroma. "I've converted more people to craft beer with our porter than with any of our other beers. I ask people, 'Are you feeling adventurous? This beer will change your life.'"

Gulf Islands offers one other bottled beer, a winter warmer called Fireside Ale. A 7 per cent ABV English-style ale, it has just enough bitterness to provide a contrast to the rich fruit and malt flavours.

Two beers are available on draft on Salt Spring Island and in a few Vancouver Island pubs and restaurants. Whaletail Ale is a German-style *alt*. Hops contribute citrus notes and a noticeable bitterness while the malts provide biscuity, toffee, and caramel flavours. India Pale Ale is a cross between a West Coast and an English IPA. The bitterness level—at sixty-five IBUs—and the alcohol level—at 6 per cent ABV—are fairly high. "But the malts give it a fullness and mellowness," Hunter said.

Heatherdale Ale, made with the petals of heather flowers, is the most unusual of the beers Hunter brews. "It's an ancient Scottish recipe, going back for centuries. I asked the people at Butchart Gardens [fifteen kilometres north of Victoria] if they would be interested in my brewing an ale that used their flowers and that they could sell in their restaurant. It's lightly hopped so that the heather aroma emerges. There are hints of vanilla in the taste." As of 2010, Heatherdale Ale was available only on draft at Butchart Gardens. However, Hunter is considering bottling it.

Merecroft Village Pub

205 – 489 South Dogwood St, Campbell River, V9W 6K6, 250-286-4944

Surgenor Brewing Company

861 Shamrock Pl, Comox, V9M 4G4, 250-339-9947, surgenorbrewing.ca

Fat Cat Brewery

2 – 940 Old Victoria Rd, Nanaimo, V9R 6Z8, 250-716-2739, fatcatbrewery.com

Longwood Brewpub

5775 Turner Rd, Nanaimo, V9T 6L8, 250-729-8856, longwoodbrewpub.com

Craig Street Brew Pub

29 Craig St, Duncan, V9L 1V7, 250-737-2337, craigstreet.ca

Gulf Islands Brewing

270 Furness Rd, Salt Spring Island, V8K 1Z7, 250-653-2383

gulfislandsbrewery.com

CHAPTER TEN

Victoria's Nautic-Ales

In the 1980s and '90s, Victoria became a leader in the nascent craft-brewing industry and it continues to be one of Canada's brewing centres of excellence. In July 2010, the city had four microbreweries and three brewpubs, five of them within a ten-minute walk of the site of the old Lucky Lager plant. Each is either at the edge of or a few blocks from the sea or its inlets. Brewery names like Canoe, Spinnakers, Driftwood, and Lighthouse, and beers called Sea Dog, Race Rocks, Fog Fighter, and Riptide are reminders of Victoria's maritime character.

❖

Driftwood Brewing Company was founded in 2008 by three young men who felt that there was room for a new brewery in Victoria's already crowded microbrewing scene. Jason Meyer had worked at Alley Kat Brewing in Edmonton and at McAuslan Brewing in Montreal before signing on with Victoria's Lighthouse Brewery. With the encouragement of Lighthouse owner Paul Hoyne, Meyer and fellow employee Kevin Hearsum experimented with different recipes in the company's small test brewery. The two of them, along with Gary Lindsay, another Lighthouse employee, often talked about starting their own brewery.

Since his homebrewing days, Meyer had enjoyed improvising on recipes he'd used and creating new ones so that he could brew beers that complemented the foods he liked. Reading the books of the late Michael Jackson, a writer who celebrated different, often little-known beer styles from around the world, he discovered Belgian beers. Flavourful, good with food, and a change from the familiar English and German styles, they didn't rigidly follow style guidelines and recipes. This was the kind of experimentation and creativity Meyer and Hearsum enjoyed. They had found their niche. "The people of Victoria had been enjoying a range of really good beers for a quarter of a century; they had developed very discriminating palates. We felt

DRIFTWOOD
ALE

DRIFTWOOD
BREWERY

CRAFT BREWED IN VICTORIA, BC.
102-450 Hillside Ave, V8T 1Y7
Beer/Biere 650 mL

In 2008, three former employees of Lighthouse Brewing, Gary Lindsay, Kevin Hearsum, and Jason Meyer (left to right), opened Driftwood Brewing, a microbrewery specializing in Belgian-style ales. The tap handles behind the three, as well as those supplied to restaurants and pubs, use pieces of driftwood collected on local beaches.

that they would be prepared to accept something new, even if the styles were centuries old."

However, the first beer Driftwood offered in the fall of 2008 was Meyer's version of a pale ale, a style that has been popular in Victoria since Spinnakers opened in 1984. Driftwood Ale, golden to light amber, makes generous use of both Northwest and German hops. The refreshing, citrusy notes are balanced by the malt which contributes a dry, not too sweet character.

Before the end of the year, Meyer and Hearsum had created two Belgian-style beers. White Bark Wheat Ale is a straw-coloured, unfiltered beer. Curaçao orange peel from the West Indies contributes a crisp, clean taste, while the wheat malt gives the beer a slightly chewy but very smooth mouth-feel. With Farmhand Ale, they moved into what, for most Victoria drinkers, was new territory. This dark gold, 5.5 per cent ABV beer, is a *saison*, or farmhouse ale, traditionally brewed in Belgium for consumption by field workers during the hot summer months. It has a tartness and a spicy taste, contributed in part by the fresh-ground pepper it contains. The yeasts—"Belgian beers are all about the yeasts," Hearsum explained—contribute fruity notes to the complex flavours.

The fourth of Driftwood's year-round beers, Crooked Coast Amber Ale, is a German-style *alt* beer. Amber in colour, it balances the aromas and taste of German hops and malts. There is a faint coffee aroma, and a slight hop bitterness. Chocolatey flavours are balanced by the citrusy characteristics of the hops. Like the three other Driftwood mainstays, this one achieves a delicate interrelationship among the various flavour notes and aromas.

Hearsum and Meyer's love of experimentation is seen in their special release beers. Blackstone Porter is a dry English porter in which "a partial sour mash lends a subtle tartness to the bittersweet chocolate flavour." Naughty Hildegard Extra Special Bitter makes generous use of Northwest hops and then balances their effect with English malts. Old Cellar Dweller Barley Wine uses "three times the malt bill and five times the hops of a normal-strength beer." It weighs in at a very high 12 per cent ABV. Brother Bart's Belgian Brown Ale, a 7.5 per cent ABV *dubbel*, and Belle Royale Belgian Strong Cherry Ale, a 9 per cent ABV fruit beer, are two of Driftwood's ventures into lesser-known styles.

"In the 1980s, the early microbrewers were seen as radical; now we are," Meyer commented. "But if we're to succeed, we have to set our standards high—not sell something just different, but something of high quality." With first-year sales of twelve hundred hectolitres and 2010 sales nearly doubling that, Driftwood appears to have provided Victoria and Vancouver Island beer drinkers with both difference and quality.

❖

After Labatt closed the Lucky Lager plant, then Victoria mayor Peter Pollen approached a group of Victoria businessmen about opening a locally owned brewery in the now-vacant building. However, Labatt, wanting to keep competition for its beer to a minimum, demolished the structure. John Hellemond, one of the investors Pollen had approached, then gathered a group of investors to build a new brewery in Saanichton, north of Victoria.

Ralf Pittroff (left), Vancouver Island's brewmaster, discusses
test results with Mike Hay, quality control supervisor.

Island Pacific Brewery, renamed **Vancouver Island Brewery** in 1992,
opened in 1985, when Goldstream Lager appeared on the market. It
was a European lager, a crossover beer to be sold on draft to both pubs
and restaurants, which, at that time, was a problem. Only bottled beers
could be sold at restaurants. However, the company successfully lob-
bied the provincial government for a change in the regulations, and
that year the brewery produced and sold over thirty-five hundred hectolitres of beer, most of it delivered to customers in an old ambulance.

Frank Appleton had helped to set up the brewery and develop the
first beer. However, it soon became apparent that a full-time brewer was
necessary. German-trained Hermann Hoerterer was hired late in 1985
and developed Island Pacific's second two beers: Hermann's Bavarian
Lager and Piper's Pale Ale. The two are still on the brewery's core list,
the former as Hermann's Dark Lager. Sales grew steadily both on the
island and in the Lower Mainland and, by 1992, the various brands
became available in 350-millilitre bottles. "We reached a wide range of
beer drinkers," remembered Barry Fisher, who served as CEO from 1988

to 2008. "People at the University of Victoria Faculty Club would be drinking Hermann's Dark Lager and at a bar downtown, younger professionals would have our regular lager, which was certainly more flavourful than the mainstream products available."

By 1995, the Saanichton facilities, which had twice been renovated, were unable to keep up with the increased demand and the decision was made to move into downtown Victoria, just a few blocks north of where the old Lucky Lager plant had been. Five years later, the company decided to offer the beers in cans; however, because the brewery didn't have a canning line, truckloads of product were transported to Prince George to be packaged by Pacific Western Brewery. In 2006, the company installed its own canning line.

Vancouver Island currently offers four year-round beers and occasional seasonal and special issue brews. "Because we are a large brewery [one of the ten largest in western Canada], we do not have the luxury of creating small brews," commented Ralf Pittroff, a German-trained brewer who visited Vancouver Island Brewery on a Canadian holiday and returned to work there in 1995. "We produce twenty thousand hectolitres a year of our main brands and that uses all of our equipment." Given the fact that many of Vancouver Island's customers are crossover drinkers with limited experience with microbrewed styles, offering something too different can be tricky. "We tried a wheat beer a few years ago and a lot of people didn't like it. It was the same colour as the beer they drank, but it tasted very different." And Hermann's Dark Lager, certainly a beer of a different colour, was approached cautiously by many drinkers. "We had to tell them not to be afraid of the dark," Pittroff joked.

Vancouver Islander Lager, the latest in a series of lagers that began with Goldstream Lager, is a 5 per cent ABV North American pale lager created for someone familiar with mainstream beers. Although, as is the case with all Vancouver Island beers, it does not include adjuncts like mainstream ones do, it is like mainstream lagers in its very mild flavour profile. There is little noticeable hop presence, and the malts create a decided sweetness.

Piper's Pale Ale, named after Piper James Richardson, a Victorian who was killed during the First World War, has long been the brewery's best seller. Pittroff described it as a West Coast-style pale ale, "but

not so hoppy." Although the bitterness level is only twenty-eight, this medium-bodied beer has a crisp hop flavour and clean finish. Moderately carbonated, it is maltier than many examples of the style. Caramel and chocolate notes more than offset the mild hop bitterness.

Hermann's Dark Lager has been well received by fans of craft brews. This 5.5 per cent ABV beer has been variously categorized as a *dunkel* and as a *schwarzbier*, two dark German styles. Opaque, almost black in colour, it is medium-bodied and low in carbonation. The chocolate and coffee tastes of the dark malts dominate, leaving almost no trace of hops.

Skyhopper Honey Brown (named after orca whales' habit of rising from the water to look around) began as a seasonal beer celebrating Vancouver Island's twenty-fifth anniversary and became so popular that it is now on the core list. It's amber in colour, its sweetness created by both the malts and the touch of local honey used in the brewing. A very slight hop note prevents the sweetness from becoming cloying. Light-bodied and smooth, it has been praised for its "drinkability."

During 2010, Vancouver Island celebrated the one hundredth anniversary of the Canadian navy by creating Sea Dog, a fairly hoppy amber ale that is based on the characteristics of German *alt* beer. "We had to call it an amber ale, not an alt, because people might not understand and think it has been in the tanks or on the shelves too long," Pittroff noted. Crystal, chocolate and honey malts give the beer a rich flavour profile. Hermannator Ice Bock, a regular winter offering, is a 9 per cent ABV beer that is created by freezing some of the water content and then removing the ice. It is a rich, malty beer, with tastes of plum.

❖

Phillips Brewing Company, the creation of a young man who has been jokingly called microbrewing's "enfant terrible," is also on Government Street, two blocks south of Vancouver Island Brewery. Matt Phillips became interested in making beer while he was a microbiology student at Mount Allison University in Nova Scotia. "We used to take trips to New England and come home with all kinds of different and wonderful beers. I began homebrewing in the dorms," he recalled, adding that he was constantly experimenting and trying out new recipes. After graduation, he worked at Grizzly Paw Brewing Company in Canmore, Alberta,

The blue delivery van, on the steps of which Matt Phillips stands, is the successor to the blue truck that gave its name to one of Phillips Brewing's beers. When a North Vancouver brewery objected to the name's similarity to that of their company's Red Truck, Phillips renamed the beer Blue Buck.

before moving to BC and doing stints at Whistler (where he worked the night shift and taught skiing during the day) and Spinnakers in Victoria.

"I wanted to make interesting beers my own way," he said, explaining why, in 2001, he decided to start his own brewery. "I chose to stay in Victoria because the water is great for brewing and there was a very knowledgeable beer culture here. I felt there would be a market for what I wanted to try out."

The story of his progress, from the owner and sole employee of a tiny brewery to the owner of a successful, multi-award-winning one that now produces thirteen thousand five hundred hectolitres annually and employs over twenty people, is detailed on the brewery's website. The account reads like a legendary rags-to-riches saga: "It is a tale that begins with an outlandish idea, a passionate brewer and a stream of refusal." Refusal began when every bank he visited denied him a loan. Phillips, who chose to maintain his independence by not involving investors, then filled out applications for every credit card he could and maxed out all of his accounts buying used brewery equipment. He set up shop in "a modest warehouse above a metal shop . . . That would be his home and workplace for the next two years." He slept in the brewery—rolling up his bedding each morning, taking showers at a nearby gym—and began brewing. His first beers, a raspberry wheat ale, an espresso stout, and an India pale ale, hit the market in the summer of 2001. He packaged these in bottles and delivered them to customers in an old milk delivery truck that he had sanded and spray-painted blue.

The first few years saw Phillips walking the thin line "between success and bankruptcy." But business grew and, in June 2004, he moved his brewery—partly because he needed more space and partly because, after one of the tanks burst and its contents leaked into the metal shop, his landlord suggested that he should relocate. In 2005, Phillips gained national recognition as his beers won three gold medals, two silvers, and a bronze at the Canadian Brewing Awards. Business grew to four thousand hectolitres the following year. The old blue truck proved inadequate for its job and was retired.

Although retired, the blue truck was not forgotten. Like the phoenix, which gives its name to the company's lager, it rose again—this time as the name of the company's amber ale. But not for long. Red Truck Beer Company in North Vancouver protested that the name was in conflict with theirs and advised that Phillips should stop using it. "We could have won the battle, but it would have been expensive." Instead, Phillips used the sympathetic publicity the issue had created in Victoria to launch a contest to rename the beer. It became Blue Buck, and Phillips cleverly developed stories about a mythical beast after which the beer had been named.

By 2008, Phillips Brewing had become so successful that it moved into a new plant on Government Street, very near where Lucky Lager had been. "Even though Phillips has moved into a bigger facility," the website reported, "the same small kettle set-up and small-batch brewing ensures the freshest ales and lagers hit your lips on a regular basis."

The four core beers, all packaged in 341-millilitre custom-designed bottles, range from a golden lager to an amber ale. Phoenix Gold Lager, named after a brewery that had been located in what is now a ghost town in the interior of BC, is a clean, crisp, highly carbonated Bohemian lager, brewed with American and Czech hops. A slight malt sweetness

complements the moderate hop bitterness. Slipstream Cream Ale is an English-style beer—mild, rich, and low in hops, with caramel flavours dominating. It is smooth and medium-bodied. "It's like an English mild ale," Phillips noted, adding that he has not followed the traditional recipe exactly. "Traditional guidelines can stifle creativity."

Blue Buck Ale and different variations on the brewery's India Pale Ale are the top-selling Phillips beers. Blue Buck is an amber beer that is highlighted by the balance between hops and malts. The caramel flavours of the malts are complemented by the dry, crisp hop finish. Phillips has praised its drinkability and called it the brewery's session beer. Hop Circle IPA, which was released in the spring of 2010, is a variation on the recipe used back in 2001. "We wanted to showcase the hops and used six different varieties." Although it is 6.5 per cent ABV and the hop bitterness registers at eighty IBUs, it is not what some people refer to as an "in-your-face beer" because the floral, citrusy aromas and taste make it tart rather than bitter.

"We see ourselves as celebrating the diversity of beer styles and brew a wide variety of beers," Phillips said, commenting on the character of the brewery. "We put out a different beer every three weeks. These are our niche beers." This diversity and variety are easily seen in an examination of the special and seasonal releases, which are packaged in 650-millilitre bottles. "They'd be slow moving as six-packs, but singles have visibility on liquor store shelves and move quickly. We make them in small batches so that they're gone before they can lose their freshness."

Among the special releases are a Belgian *tripel*, a German *dunkel*, an Imperial red ale, an Imperial stout, a *doppelbock*, a pumpkin ale, a ginger ale, and a chocolate porter. Often the alcohol level is high; one list of Phillips beers shows eleven offerings over 7 per cent ABV. The names are catchy or perhaps, as one person has called them, cheeky: Dr. Funk Dunkel, Instigator Doppelbock, Dirty Squirrel Hazelnut Brown Ale, GrowHop Fresh Hop Bitter, Amnesiac Double IPA, and Surly Blonde Big Belgian Tripel. The names on the bottle labels catch the eye of potential buyers; the quality of the beer inside has customers asking the brewery when the various special releases will be reintroduced.

Andrew Tessier, whose brews have won twenty-one Canadian Brewing Awards, explains the beer menu to a customer in the brewpub of Swans Suite Hotel.

Opened in 1989, the brewpub at **Swans Suite Hotel** is the second-oldest continuously operating brewpub in BC. Just east of Victoria's Johnson Street Bridge and a ten-minute walk from Phillips, the brewpub came about through the vision of the late Michael Williams, a one-time sheep rancher and dog trainer who had renovated two adjacent heritage buildings in downtown Victoria. In the mid-1980s, he purchased an empty 1913 warehouse that had been the home of Buckerfield's Farm Supplies, a store he had once patronized, and turned it into an upscale apartment building with stores on the main floor. However, when an economic slowdown occurred near the end of the decade, he approached the government for authorization to turn the main floor into a brewpub. His application was denied, but one official suggested that, should he turn the apartments into hotel rooms, he would qualify for a pub licence.

The upper floors became an elegant suite hotel, its rooms decorated with the work of local artists, and the main floor became the brewpub. The walls were not hung with television sets, but with works from Williams's personal art collection, which included many pieces by contemporary West Coast First Nations artists. Hanging baskets and vases of flowers brighten the environment on gloomy Victoria days. Entertainment consists of conversation and listening to local musicians.

The brewery, which was called Buckerfield's after the feed store, and was set up by Frank Appleton, is in the back of this building that used to store grains. The original brewers, brothers Sean and Paul Hoyne, put grains to other uses. Sean moved on in the mid-1990s to start the brewery at Canoe Brewpub, just up the street, and Paul started Lighthouse Brewing in nearby Esquimalt. Since 2003, Andrew Tessier, who has been referred to as the wunderkind of microbrewing, has been the brewer. A local boy, he and a group of teenaged friends formed a club they called The Raging Grainies and set up a brewery in the basement of the Tessier home. "My parents were very supportive. One time a local homebrew supplier wouldn't sell ingredients to me because he thought I was too young. The next day my dad, who didn't drink, came in with me and bought the supplies."

To Tessier, brewing is an art. "There has to be a scientific base but until the last thirty years, the art was mainly ignored." Certainly, his work at Swans has demonstrated that Tessier is an artist. Since 2003, he has won twenty-one Canadian Brewing Awards: ten gold medals, seven silvers, and four bronze. In 2006 alone, he took home five golds, two silvers, and a bronze. What is amazing, in addition to the number of awards, is the variety of styles for which they have been given—eleven in all, ranging from a Bavarian lager to an Extra IPA.

Tessier characterizes his beers as being in the English style, full-bodied and flavourful. "They're unfiltered, unpasteurized, and fresh, especially when they're served on draft." He noted that they're also available at the Swans beer and wine store next door and at private liquor stores on Vancouver Island and in Vancouver. "The private stores keep the beer in coolers and away from fluorescent light. This preserves their freshness."

The range of styles offered at the brewpub is important, as it allows patrons to discover how different beers match with different foods. And, when someone orders a Lucky, "We suggest they try our taster nest so that they realize just how many different kinds of really flavourful beers there are." Tessier began describing his beers by talking about Old Towne

Bavarian Lager, Arctic Ale, Pandora Pale Ale, and Smooth Sailing Honey Ale, all of which are mild, session-type beers, ideal for newcomers to craft beer. The 5 per cent ABV lager he defines as a cross between a German pilsner and a *helles*, more full-bodied than the former, but with a note of hop bitterness. Fully carbonated, it has a soft, smooth texture. Arctic Ale, the brewpub's top seller, is an English summer ale: clean, crisp, and mildly hopped. The addition of some wheat malt provides smoothness. Pandora Pale Ale, which like Arctic is a 4.5 per cent ABV beer, is an English-style pale, not too hoppy. Tessier referred to the "happy medium" between the hops and the malts. While both hop bitterness and malt sweetness are evident, each of these qualities is subtle rather than overwhelming. The name for Smooth Sailing came from Tessier's homebrewing buddies, who always looked forward to the latest batch of his honey beer. He noted that the honey is put into the wort so that its sugars are fermented. The resulting beer is thus not too sweet and any sweetness there is is balanced by the mild hop finish.

With Appleton Brown, Extra Special Bitter, and Extra IPA, Tessier offers his interpretations of three classic English styles. The brown, named after the microbrewing pioneer, uses roasted chocolate malts that provide smoothness and rich malty flavours. The ESB is a copper-coloured beer that balances a robust, creamy, malt flavour with a crisp hop finish. The IPA, which weighs in at 6.8 per cent ABV, is "specially brewed for the hop lover" and the hop bitterness, aromas, and flavours work together.

Tessier's other award-winning creations include Berry Ale (7 per cent ABV) to which raspberries are added during fermentation; Riley's Scotch Ale (8 per cent ABV), which balances hops and malts; and Oatmeal Stout (5.4 per cent ABV), which uses seven varieties of malts and oats.

❖

When Sean Hoyne left Swans to start up the brewery at **Canoe Brewpub, Marina and Restaurant,** he had only to head a block and a half north. One of three homebrewing brothers, he'd studied biochemistry and microbiology at Montreal's Vanier College before switching to English and coming to Victoria to study for a Master's degree in modern Irish literature. After he finished his literary studies, he began a brewing

Executive chef Alain Leger (left) and brewmaster
Sean Hoyne discuss beer and food pairings for Canoe.

apprenticeship under Frank Appleton, became head brewer at Swans, and hired his brother Paul.

"This building is one of our greatest assets," Hoyne remarked about the home of Canoe Brewpub, an 1894 heritage building that originally housed the electrical plant for downtown Victoria. The building underwent six million dollars of renovations before the brewpub opened in 1996. The original brick walls and fir posts were retained and give a rustic atmosphere to the brewpub and restaurant. There is a pool table and some televisions that are "more off than on." Twice a week, local musicians provide the entertainment. Outside, a warm-weather patio overlooks a small marina that is part of the establishment. "The whole package is what we offer," Hoyne explained. "The building, the view, the food, the music, and the beer."

The beer, which Hoyne neither filters nor pasteurizes, is designed, in part, to complement the food. Red Canoe Lager, for example, can be paired with the organic greens; Beaver Brown Ale with the baby back ribs. Unlike Swans or Spinnakers, which have a large number of

8.0

year-round beer offerings, Canoe has only four. Hoyne described each as being distinct from the other three and as being a classic example of its style—with an occasional tweak. "I do a lot of reading about the backgrounds of each style, including traditional recipes, and then try well-known examples." When asked if this approach parallelled the technique Irish writer James Joyce used in his masterpiece *Ulysses*, which was, among many other things, a modern interpretation of a traditional epic and its conventions, he smiled and agreed.

Red Canoe Lager, in spite of its Canadian-themed label illustration, is a Vienna lager, a light gold beer that balances a light malt sweetness with a clean-finishing hop flavour. "It's as authentic a German lager as I can make," Hoyne commented. Siren's Song Pale Ale, which makes reference to the dangerous females whose enchanting songs threatened to lure legendary Greek hero Odysseus to his death, is "our answer to the West Coast-style pale ale." Light amber and light- to medium-bodied, it is more hopped than English versions of the style, although the hops do not overwhelm the malt flavours and add their own tastes and aroma.

Hops are more noticeable in River Rock Bitter, an English extra special bitter that is "our least popular beer over all, but one that inspires the fiercest dedication and loyalty among its fans. It's meant to help local Brits dream of home." Even though it is well-hopped, it has a substantial malt profile that provides a complex variety of flavours. Beaver Brown Ale, another English classic in spite of the Canadian name, is Canoe's most popular regular beer. "It's darker than most English browns," Hoyne observed. "It's close to being a porter." Rich but not sweet coffee and chocolate malt flavours dominate this mahogany-coloured, smooth, medium-bodied beer.

The five seasonal beers are Habit Espresso Stout, a winter brew that includes espresso from a local coffee producer; Winter Gale IPA, a 6.3 per cent ABV winter warmer to which cinnamon, cloves, nutmeg, and ginger are added; Bavarian Copper Bock; Black Cherry Porter, a dessert beer infused with cherry juice; and Summer Honey Wheat Ale.

Paul Hoyne set up **Lighthouse Brewing Company** two kilometres west of Swans in an industrial area in Esquimalt. Before coming to Victoria,

Paul Hoyne founded Lighthouse Brewing because he saw an opportunity
for a Victoria microbrewery that offered products farther away
from the mainstream than those of Vancouver Island Brewery.

he'd worked for Ontario breweries and brewpubs in Port Credit, Don
Mills, and Toronto, acquiring a sound training in brewing classical
English and German styles. He and his founding partner, Gerry Hieter,
who had started Whistler Brewing, realized that there was a market

for a second brewery in Victoria. "Vancouver Island was creating fairly mainstream beers. Local drinkers had been developing a taste for micro-brewed beers because of Spinnakers, Swans, and Canoe, but those were not [yet] available off-premises."

Lighthouse Brewing, the name of which was chosen to celebrate the buildings that played so large a role in the area's maritime history, began brewing in 1998. On August 17 of that year, Lighthouse sold its first keg, Race Rocks Ale, an English-style, amber beer. "It was a style not available in this area, but I knew that Victoria would be a good market for it." Race Rocks and later, Beacon IPA, Keepers Stout, and the simply named Lager, developed a strong following on the southern part of the island and, in 2004, the company installed a canning line. "Cans were less expensive than bottles and easier to transport, they kept the beer fresher, and they were environmentally friendly." Sales doubled over the next year. In 2007, when a new canning line was set up, production increased fivefold. Then in 2009, Hoyne and his partners made the decision to install a bottling line, reversing the usual progression at microbreweries. Not only would they now be able to offer their core brands to hard-core bottle aficionados, they would also be able to create limited, special edition beers. They wouldn't have to order enormous quantities of specially labelled cans, just labels to put on bottles. Annual production grew to twelve thousand hectolitres in 2010.

When asked to describe Lighthouse beers, general manager Michael Bierman emphasized that the goal is to create "a quality product." He added, with a smile, "We hope we're a little craftier than the rest of the BC breweries." Hoyne was more specific: "We're not trying to shock or threaten drinkers, but to make really flavourful beers. We like to be true to traditional styles and to offer them to as many drinkers as possible. Our beers are balanced; we don't want to showcase only one ingredient. Our yeasts enhance the characteristics of the hops and malts we use."

The recipes of the four core Lighthouse beers are, Hoyne has said, "written in stone." Although some slight tweaking might occur, the object has been to create beers that are consistent from brew to brew, flavourful, and familiar to drinkers. Race Rocks Ale, a 5.2 per cent ABV amber ale, features chocolate and crystal malts. Chestnut in colour, it is smooth and medium-bodied. Beacon IPA, an English-style 5.3 per cent ABV copper-coloured beer, is not over-hopped. "The Simpson malts from England and the Willamette Valley hops from Oregon balance each other. You could call it a session IPA." Keepers is a dry, Irish-style stout, full-bodied and creamy, with espresso, chocolate, and roasted notes. Clean finishing, it does not have the malty sweetness that is found in other Lighthouse beers. Lighthouse Lager was created to meet a market demand. "People wanted to support locally made products," Hoyne noted, "but a lot of them were lager drinkers. So we produced an all-natural alternative to mainstream brands." Like the brewery's other core brands, the lager achieves a balance between the slight sweetness of the malts and the clean, crisp finish of the hops.

Since the introduction of the bottling line in 2009, the four core brands have been available in both bottles and cans, as well as on draft. Two new core brands are available in bottles, but not cans. Riptide Pale Ale is, as Hoyne described it, "an unusual pale ale but there is no shock. It's very drinkable, partly because we use orange peel for a citrus flavour." Fisgard 150 Lager, named to celebrate the 150th anniversary of BC's oldest lighthouse, is a Bavarian-style lager that is a cross between a *helles* and a pilsner, sharing the sweeter malt notes of the former and the crispness and floral notes of the latter.

❖

Spinnakers Gastro Brewpub, the first self-contained and the longest continuously operating brewpub in Canada, is a ten-minute walk from Swans—across the Johnson Street Bridge, along Esquimalt Road and then south to the foot of Catherine Street. Someone who hadn't visited the establishment at the edge of Victoria's outer harbour since 1984 would be impressed with the changes that have taken place, both around and within the building. What was once an aging and shabby district is populated with high-end condominiums, and a walking and jogging trail follows the seashore.

The heritage house that was initially the brewpub has grown. Inside the entrance, a small gift shop offers malt vinegar brewed on premises, bottled mineral water from a well sunk on the property, locally produced baked goods and chocolates, and glasses and other souvenirs. The brewpub has been relocated to a second-floor addition and now seats a hundred and eighteen people, ninety-eight inside and twenty on a patio. High ceilings, dark-panelled walls, a wood-burning fireplace, two pool tables, and two dart boards give the feel of an old English pub, but one with spectacular views of the outer harbour, the Strait of Juan de Fuca and the Olympic Mountains. Oh, yes—there are televisions, three of them. The ground floor, the original location of the brewpub, is now a gourmet restaurant—or gastropub, to use the appropriate terminology—that seats a hundred and five inside and another sixty on the outdoor patio.

Beyond the main building are guest rooms and suites in a restored 1884 heritage house and a modern bungalow. A few blocks to the north, Spinnakers Spirit Merchants offers a large selection of hard-to-find wines and a variety of BC microbrews. A second store, James Bay Spirit Merchants, is in another historic district and Sips Artisan Bistro, next door to the James Bay store, offers pairings of BC wines and local artisan foods.

The expansion and growth of Spinnakers came about, explained Paul Hadfield, one of the original owners, because he and his partners realized that, by itself, a sixty-five-seat neighbourhood pub could not generate enough revenue to be profitable, even if it offered pleasant surroundings, a spectacular view, and very good food and beer. In fact, even as the pub opened on May 15, 1984, changes were planned. On Wednesday, May 16, 1984, the *Times Colonist* carried a short article announcing that the one-day-old establishment had submitted applications to the city for permission to buy adjoining property so that the pub could expand.

Bringing about some of the later changes involved challenging existing city and provincial laws. "I remember when we were going to open the restaurant," Hadfield remarked, "we needed a separate liquor licence from the one we had for the brewpub. And at first, they made objections to the fact that the beer would be brewed in the same building as the restaurant, which wasn't allowed. We thought we might have to load kegs of the beer onto a truck, drive it out of and back into the parking lot and then deliver the kegs to the restaurant." The law was changed.

Throughout its over a quarter of a century of operation, what has distinguished Spinnakers, making it much more than just another neighbourhood pub with a good view and good food, has been the beer. The pioneering brewing of John Mitchell, whose three original beers—

Paul Hadfield, co-founder and co-owner of Spinnakers, enjoys a beer with assistant brewer Tommy Grant and brewmaster Rob Monk.

Spinnakers Ale, John Mitchell's ESB, and Mt. Tolmie Dark—are still regularly brewed, has been followed by the work of people who began at Spinnakers and then went on to distinguished careers elsewhere. The list includes Barry Ladell of Nanaimo's Longwood Brewpub, Mike Tymchuk of Calgary's Wild Rose Brewery and Matt Phillips, who moved a few blocks away from Spinnakers to start his award-winning eponymous brewery.

"We're still primarily an ale house, although we occasionally do a lager, and we've expanded beyond our English roots," Hadfield noted. "The original three beers were different from what people were used to in 1984, but they weren't far out. We've experimented with a variety of styles as people's palates have developed. We encourage our brewers to have fun, to be aggressive when they want to be, and to make interesting beers." He spoke of the production of a number of Belgian styles, which, although they are centuries old, have only recently become popular with North American craft-brew drinkers. Among these are a blonde ale, an abbey ale, a strong ale, a *saison*, and a *lambic*.

Much of the interest in the beers comes from the often-unusual ingredients added to familiar styles. There has been a basil IPA, a rosewater IPA, a chai-vanilla stout, a cranberry-orange-zest ale, and a saffron-honey pale ale. Frequently these beers, which give the brewers a chance to exercise their imaginations and creativity, are brewed in very small batches and served in fifteen- or thirty-litre casks that are carried from the cellar to the bar late each weekday afternoon. The fun often comes from such names as King Tut's Tipple, Titanic Stout, Iceberg Pale Ale, and Unsinkable Molly Brown Ale, each of which was applied to a beer created to celebrate special exhibits at Victoria's Royal British Columbia Museum.

The current brewmaster is Rob Monk, who learned the trade at Whitehorse's Yukon Brewery, starting in the gift shop, then working on the bottling line, and finally moving to assisting in the brewing. He applied for work at Spinnakers when he moved to Victoria with his girlfriend. "I met brewer Lon Ladell [Barry's son] and we chatted. They offered me part-time work doing odd jobs around the brewery. Later, I became assistant brewmaster, and in 2006, I took over the main job. Coming to Victoria opened my eyes to a whole new world of brewing. I've really become interested in the Belgian tradition. I learn something new every day, not just in the brewery but when I talk to our regulars— they aren't shy about asking hard questions and even offering some hard criticism. In a way, we're beer nerds making beer for other beer nerds."

Monk adds a qualifier. "The goal at Spinnakers is to make rounded beers, beers that are well-balanced. You should experience the expected flavours. We want a brewery you can count on at all times. That doesn't mean we're timid, but we don't want to brew something that's in your face. We take pride in what we do; we put a lot of ourselves into the product. If there's a distinguishing quality to our beers, it's probably in the complexity of the malt profiles."

The bar operates nine taps: four or five beers from the year-round list, a couple of rotating seasonal beers, and a special edition beer, along with Merridale Cider, produced in the Vancouver Island village of Cobble Hill, and O de Vie, a lightly carbonated mineral water that uses water from the brewery's on-site well. There are five main beers. Nut Brown Ale is a mildly hopped traditional English brown, in which the chocolatey and roasty flavour of the malts is balanced by Saaz hops. John Mitchell's ESB, one of the grand originals, is low in carbonation and served at cellar temperature. It is low in bitterness and offers a complex

TITANIC

TITANIC

TITANIC

TITANIC
STRONG STOUT

...d after the classic Imperial Stouts brewed around the shipyards of England, this is a strong stout, refined, rich and aromatic, to withstand the rigors of traveling long distances.

...REFULLY, IN A SINGLE MOTION, LEAVING THE LAST CENTIMETER ...XIMUM SHELF LIFE, STORE IN A COOL DARK PLACE.

variety of malt flavours. Spinnakers IPA is a 7.1 per cent ABV English-style ale in which the assertive hop character is prevented from being "in your face" by the malt body. At 8 per cent ABV, Blue Bridge Double IPA is a more adventurous brew, assertively hopped in the West Coast style, while by contrast, Spinnakers Ale, an English mild, is light-bodied and lightly hopped, with a slightly sweet malt finish. An oatmeal stout and a traditional English porter are offered on a rotating basis; Fog Fighter, a yeasty, strong Belgian ale, is brewed for the winter months, and a *hefeweizen* for the warmer weather.

If patrons take a fancy to one of the regular or rotating beers, they can buy a 650-millilitre bottle from the cooler at the end of the bar. But they shouldn't look for any of them at either of the two Spinnakers liquor stores: provincial liquor regulations prevent breweries from selling their own products at liquor stores they own.

Driftwood Brewing Company
    102 - 450 Hillside Ave, Victoria, V8T 1Y7, 250-384-2333, driftwoodbeer.com
Vancouver Island Brewery
    2330 Government St, Victoria, V8T 5G5, 250-361-0007, vanislandbrewery.com
Phillips Brewing Company
    2010 Government St, Victoria, V8T 4P1, 250-380-1912, phillipsbeer.com
Swans Suite Hotel/Buckerfield's Brewery
    506 Pandora Ave, Victoria, V8W 1N6, 250-361-3310, swanshotel.com
Canoe Brewpub, Marina and Restaurant
    450 Swift St, Victoria, V8W 1S3, 250-361-1940, canoebrewpub.com
Lighthouse Brewing Company
    2 - 836 Devonshire Rd, Victoria, V9A 4T4, 250-383-6500, lighthousebrewing.com
Spinnakers Gastro Brewpub
    308 Catherine St, Victoria, V9A 3S8, 250-386-2739, spinnakers.com

Afterword
That's Ale, Folks!

When I told an inquiring neighbour that the book I was about to send the publishers would be called *Beer Quest West*, he asked about the object of my quest. Was I searching for the ideal pub or the perfect pint, he wondered. And did I find either of them? I explained that my quest was for neither. I wasn't looking for either a Shangri-La for beer drinkers or a Holy Grail filled with a perfect blend of water, malt, hops, and yeasts. The quest was to learn about and experience different kinds of lagers and ales.

After nearly two years of reading, interviewing, and tasting, I found out that there was both a fluidity and a consistency to the beer industry. There were frequent shifts in ownership. In November 2008, Labatt, which had been foreign-owned since the 1990s, became a part of a larger international conglomerate that included Anheuser-Busch of the United States. Labatt joined Molson and Sleeman as large Canadian breweries that had been swallowed by even larger multinational companies. During the two years, eleven new microbreweries and pubs opened and three others expanded or announced expansion plans. Two brewpubs closed and Molson Coors, part of the Miller-Coors-Molson-South African-Brewery conglomerate, purchased Granville Island.

In the brewhouses themselves, there was also fluidity. Traditional English ales and German lagers continued to be made, but young and talented brewers experimented with variations on old styles and created new ones. Ginger, heather, hibiscus, and spruce joined honey, raspberry, and cherry as additives, giving new flavour notes to familiar styles. Several microbrewers began experimenting with lagers, which they admitted were more difficult and unforgiving to create than ales. Beers using wheat malt along with barley malt became popular with craft-beer drinkers. Several brewers introduced little-known Belgian styles that were received with great enthusiasm.

Since the mid-1980s, Molson and Labatt had also introduced "new" beers—light, dry, ice, and low-carb to name four. But many experienced and cynical drinkers remarked that these were just new wrinkles on the pale North American lagers that had dominated the market for decades. Consistency was an essential element of the megabrewers' making and marketing of beers: Bud or Molson Canadian or Coors Light was expected to taste the same no matter where or when it was consumed. As it is for the huge hamburger chains, only controlled surprises were permitted. By contrast, many microbrewers, especially those working for brewpubs, spoke of listening and responding to customer feedback, tweaking their beers to create more interesting flavours, and sometimes pushing style envelopes as far as they could.

I discovered that there were other important constants, not just the essential sameness of each megabrewer's North American lager. The first was that opening and successfully operating a microbrewery or brewpub was hard work. There needed to be a lot of start-up capital and, because of the relatively small size of the operations, costs per unit of beer were far higher than for the megabrewers.

Selling their product was also a challenge. Without the enormous advertising budgets of brewers like Molson Coors and Labatt, and the high-profile sponsorship of major league sports telecasts those budgets allowed, microbrewers had to find creative ways of reaching the beer-drinking public—often, as one brewer said, glass by glass, one drinker at a time. In addition to giving tastings at bars, liquor stores, and beer festivals, these small breweries become involved in the communities where they were located, helping local artists and musicians and amateur sports teams. They also used creativity, coming up with attention-getting nicknames like Pompous Pompadour, Idiot Rock, and Amnesiac.

. Another constant was the pride and passion the microbrewers brought to their work. They came from many backgrounds. Most had been homebrewers and some had trained at internationally recognized brewing schools, but many learned on the job, leaving other occupations to earn a living doing what they loved. During my travels, I met a former apprentice stonemason and a former architecture intern, a classical history student and an English major, some civil servants, a motorcycle mechanic, and an oil rig worker. Several admitted that they could have made more money if they'd followed their earlier career paths, but that they wouldn't trade their present professions for any other. They liked creatively brewing a variety of beers and working to make them as good as they possibly could. They liked drinking their own beers and sharing them with others.

Over nearly two years, I had the opportunity to sample several versions of well over sixty beer styles. They had interesting tastes and a great deal of flavour. Each brewer's treatment of a specific style was unique. Most of beers were very good, some were excellent. Only a few of them were like pale North American lager, the "beer" I'd consumed for the first quarter of a century of my legal beer-drinking years. Thank goodness!

Because of what I learned and experienced during my "Beer Quest West," I now realize that it has no specific end. As long as the brewers of Alberta and British Columbia continue to create so many different and wonderful lagers and ales, mine will be a "Never-Ending Beer Quest West."

Glossary of Brewing Terms

This short list—just over a baker's dozen of six-packs—is designed to give brief definitions of some essential terms relating to beer and brewing. For readers wishing to develop a truly extensive and impressive vocabulary on the subject, Dan Rabin and Carl Forget's *A Dictionary of Beer and Brewing* (2nd edition) is essential. It contains over 2,500 terms. Descriptions of specific beer styles can be found in Appendix III.

ABV: abbreviation for alcohol by volume.

ABW: abbreviation for alcohol by weight.

additive: an ingredient added to the wort during or after the boiling process to add flavours. Popular additives include fruits or fruit extracts and spices.

adjunct: corn, rice, or another unmalted cereal grain that is a source of fermentable sugar and can be substituted for malted grain (usually barley) in the brewing process. Beers brewed with adjuncts are paler in colour and lighter in body. Beer purists complain that megabrewers use adjuncts to cut costs and that the finished products lack taste.

aftertaste: taste and feel on the tongue after swallowing a mouthful of beer.

ale: one of the two main categories of beer (the other is lager). Ales are created with top-fermenting yeast (yeast that rises to the top of the wort during the fermentation process). They are fermented at temperatures of between sixteen and twenty degrees Celsius and are usually darker, fuller bodied, and more robust in flavour than lagers.

alcohol by volume: in Canada and England, the percentage of alcohol in beer is measured by volume; in the United States the measurement is usually by weight, which, because alcohol weighs less than water, is a lower percentage. Standard mainstream lagers are usually around 5 per cent ABV or 4 per cent alcohol by weight (ABW). Microbrewers often create beers that have higher alcohol by volume percentages, although these do not often exceed 10 per cent ABV. Occasionally, brewers have created strong (sometimes called extreme or big) beers that have even higher ABV percentages.

alcohol by weight: because alcohol weighs less than water, alcohol by weight percentages are lower than alcohol by volume percentages by approximately 20 per cent.

all-grain beer: beer brewed using only malted grains. No malt extracts (syrup made from malt) or adjuncts (such as corn or rice) are used.

barley: the cereal grain which, when malted and mashed to produce fermentable sugars, is the main ingredient of beer. The grain comes in two- and six-row varieties, the former being preferred for its higher quality.

barrel-aged: beer that is aged in wooden barrels that previously held such alcoholic beverages as port-style wine or bourbon. The beer takes on some of the flavour of those liquors.

beer: an alcoholic drink made with the fermented sugars from malted grains, usually barley, and flavoured with hops. In Spain, say "*cerveza,*" in France "*bière,*" in Italy "*birra,*" and in Germany and Holland "*bier,*" and you'll derive more enjoyment from your European travels.

body: sometimes referred to as mouth-feel, it is the tactile sensation— such as thickness or thinness of beer—in the mouth.

boutique brewery: synonym for craft brewery.

brewpub: a pub that brews its own beer mainly for consumption on the premises, although the beers are sometimes available for takeout in kegs, party pigs, growlers, or bottles.

bright beer: beer which, after primary fermentation and filtration and before packaging, is placed in a large tank for clarification, carbonation, and further maturation.

budget beer: low-priced beer, sometimes referred to by megabreweries as value-priced beer, and by beer purists in less polite terms. Frequently, budget beers are brewed with large quantities of less expensive adjuncts (such as corn and rice) replacing malted barley.

CAMRA (Campaign for Real Ale): a consumer organization that was started in England in 1971 to protest the invasion of English pubs by megabrewers supplying mass-produced pale lagers. The organization fought for the preservation of "real ale"—cask-conditioned, non-pasteurized beer. CAMRA has branches in the United States and

Canada and is credited with encouraging the Canadian microbrewing movement that began in the 1980s.

carbonation: the dissolving of carbon dioxide, a by-product of the fermentation process, into beer, creating a bubbling and foaming when a bottle is poured or a keg is tapped. Beers, such as pale lagers, designed to be served at lower temperatures are more carbonated than those served at higher temperatures.

conditioning: a secondary fermentation in which yeast is added after the beer has been transferred from fermenting tanks to kegs, casks, or bottles.

contract brewery: a company without brewing facilities that hires another brewery to produce its recipes, but then markets and sells the product itself. This arrangement allows the former to avoid the expense of purchasing equipment and the latter to operate at greater capacity. The term is sometimes used to refer to the brewery that makes the product under contract for another company.

cottage brewery: synonym for craft brewery.

craft brewery: a small brewery, producing small batches of all-malt (containing no adjuncts), unpasteurized, and sometimes unfiltered beer.

crossover beers: beers that are sufficiently similar to mainstream beers to give inexperienced drinkers an introduction to microbrewed products.

draft beer: a beer, often unpasteurized, that is served directly from a keg or cask. The term "bottled (or canned) draft beer" used by some brewers is an oxymoron.

dry beer: a beer brewed with yeasts that create a higher alcohol content and which, because there is less sugar in the finished product, is not very sweet and has very little aftertaste.

dry-hopping: adding hops late in the brewing process to enhance flavour and aroma without increasing bitterness.

drinkability: a term frequently used in the advertising of megabrewers to describe a beverage that tastes good, has a smooth texture, is easy to swallow, is non-threatening, and makes the drinker want another.

esters: compounds that are formed during fermentation and give fruity aromas and taste to beer.

extract: a syrupy or sometimes powdered concentration of wort that homebrewers often use instead of malted grains.

fermentation: the action of yeasts on the sugar in wort, producing carbon dioxide and alcohol. Bottom-fermenting yeasts are used for brewing lagers; top-fermenting yeasts for ales.

fire brewing: process of using direct fire instead of steam or hot water to boil the wort.

firkin: a 40.9-litre container. Drinkers consuming products drawn from these containers have been heard to exclaim, "This firkin beer is firkin good."

foam: the gathering of bubbles of carbon dioxide at the top of a glass or mug of beer. Aficionados judge the quality of foam by its colour, thickness, and retention period. Sometimes referred to as "suds."

green beer: freshly fermented, unconditioned beer. Also, what some people drink too much of on March 17.

growler: a 2.4-litre (half-gallon) refillable glass bottle used by many brewpubs to sell their beer for customers to take off premises.

head: the foam collected at the top of a glass or mug of beer. Also, a part of the anatomy that hurts the morning after a night of excessive imbibing.

hectolitre: one hundred litres, a standard measurement of brewing production or of the capacity of a brewing system. A hectolitre is the equivalent of just under fifty six-packs of beer.

hops: the cone-shaped flowers of a climbing vine related to cannabis that are used to provide bitterness and a variety of aromas and tastes to beer. Before the development of refrigeration, hops were added as a preservative to ales shipped from England to India.

IBU: abbreviation for International Bitterness Unit.

ice beer: a lager conditioned at temperatures sufficiently low to cause water to form ice crystals, which are then removed to give the beer a higher alcohol content.

Imperial: a term often applied to beers with high alcohol content (usually above 7 per cent ABV).

International Bitterness Unit: unit of measurement, in parts per million, of the level of bitterness contributed to beer by hop compounds. The higher the number of units, the greater the bitterness. The bitterness counteracts sweetness contributed by the malt. Pale North American lagers are low in IBUs (ten or less), while India Pale Ales are high (often sixty IBUs or more).

kraeusening: the process of introducing a small amount of fermenting wort to fully fermented beer to cause secondary fermentation and natural carbonation.

lace: patterns of foam created on the inside of a glass as the beer level goes down. Beer aficionados consider lacing to be one of the important visual qualities of beer.

lager: from the German word *lagern*, "to store," lager refers to beers that are brewed with bottom-fermenting yeasts and then stored for conditioning for longer periods and at lower temperatures than ales, usually around nine degrees Celsius. Developed in Germany, lager beers became more widely brewed with the development of refrigeration. Now the most-consumed type of beer around the world, lagers are the main products of the international megabrewers.

light beer: a beer that is low in calories and alcohol content, usually 4 per cent ABV. Many brewers label these products with the spelling "lite."

light struck: term applied to beer that has developed an unpleasant, "skunky" taste as a result of exposure to sunlight. Commercials showing sun shining on clear bottles may look romantic, but the contents would most certainly be light struck.

liquor: a term used by brewers to refer to the water used in making beer. Because the mineral content of water influences the taste of beer, it is important to have the appropriate liquor for the beer style being brewed.

malt: grain (usually barley) that is soaked in water until germination begins and then heat-dried to convert the starches in it into soluble, fermentable sugars. The length and temperature of the procedure produces different colours of malt, which create different flavours and colours in beer.

malt extract: a syrup or powder obtained from the wort. It is sometimes used instead of malt in the brewing process.

mash tun: an insulated brewing vessel in which the malted grains and water are mixed and heated.

mashing: the process of steeping ground malt in hot water to produce wort, a liquid containing soluble sugars that are converted into alcohol during the fermentation process.

microbrewery: a small brewery with an annual production of under sixty thousand hectolitres in BC, and under twenty thousand in Alberta, most of which is sold off-premises in kegs, bottles, or cans.

mouth-feel: texture of beer experienced by the mouth. Beers may be light- to full-bodied and lightly to heavily carbonated.

nitrogen: a gas which, when used instead of carbon dioxide to dispense draft beer, gives the beer a creamy texture.

nitrogen infusion: the process of putting nitrogen into beer as it is dispensed into a pitcher or glass.

nose: the aroma of freshly poured beer. Also, a part of the face that may turn red when a person consumes far too much beer at one time.

party pig: a self-pressurized plastic beer container, shaped like a pig, that holds six-and-a-half litres of beer. Brewpubs often use party pigs to sell draft beer for consumption off-premises.

pasteurization: the brief exposure of beer to high heat to kill micro-organisms and to extend bottled beer's shelf life. Many microbreweries do not pasteurize their brews, contending that the process adversely affects taste.

pitching: adding yeast to cooled wort to begin the process of fermentation.

publican: a pub or tavern's owner or manager.

real ale: unpasteurized, cask-conditioned beer served on draft.

regional brewery: bigger than a microbrewery, a regional brewery produces a larger quantity of beer and distributes its product over a much wider area. Big Rock of Calgary is considered a regional brewery.

Reinheitsgebot: the Bavarian Purity Law, enacted in 1516, which mandated that only barley malt (and later other malts), hops, water, and (after it had been identified) yeast could be used to brew beer. Although the German government repealed the law in 1987, many microbrewers advertise their adherence to the philosophy of the law. Okanagan Spring's 1516 Bavarian Lager is named after the law.

rice: a grain which, because it contains a very high percentage of starch that can be converted into fermentable sugar, is often used as an "adjunct" or substitute for more expensive barley or wheat malts.

saccrification: process of turning malt starches into fermentable sugars.

scurvy grass ale: according to the *Dictionary of Beer and Brewing*, this was a combination of watercress and ale believed to stave off scurvy. So, if you're planning a solo boat trip across the ocean . . . ?

seasonal beers: beers that are released for specific seasons. For example, pumpkin beer in the autumn and *bock* beer in the spring.

session beer: because of their low alcohol levels and smooth mouth-feel, several session beers can be consumed during an evening (a session) at a pub or tavern.

shelf life: the length of time that canned or bottled beer can be kept before beginning to spoil.

sparging: hot-water rinsing of mash after the initial separation of mash and wort. The process removes any fermentable sugars still remaining in the mash.

special edition beers: usually limited, small batches of unusual or experimental styles of beer.

style: a group of beers that share many of the same characteristics of appearance, aroma, taste, and alcohol content. (See Appendix III for discussions and examples of specific styles.)

tulipai: the *Dictionary of Beer and Brewing* defines the term as "yellow water" and as a synonym for "tiswin," a beer once brewed by the Apaches. Perhaps it might be used as a synonym for an impolite term some people use in describing adjunct-laden pale North American lagers.

value-priced beer: term used by breweries (usually megabreweries) for beers that are priced lower than the other beers they produce. Frequently, value-priced beers use a high proportion of adjuncts. See **budget beer.**

wort: (pronounced "wert"): the sugar solution created during the mashing process. The solution is boiled with hops, then cooled. Yeast then turns the sugar into alcohol and carbon dioxide.

yeast: the unicellular, microscopic organism that converts sugars in the wort into alcohol and carbon dioxide. Before it was identified, it was considered miraculous and called "Godisgood."

zymology: the scientific study of the processes of fermentation.

From Grain to Glass
Brewing, Packaging, and Drinking Beer

The Big Four: Basic Ingredients

Water, malted grain, hops, and yeast.

For centuries, these ingredients have been used to brew beer. Because there are different types of each ingredient and the four can be combined in a variety of ways, they can be used to create dozens of different styles of beer.

Water makes up at least 90 per cent of a glass or bottle of beer. Brewers call it "liquor" and five litres of it are required for each litre brewed. In addition to the water content of the product, water is used in the brewing process and in the vigorous cleaning of equipment. The relative hardness or softness of water influences the taste of the beverage and, before the twentieth century, certain styles emerged because of the composition of the water close to a brewery. The hard water of England's Burton-on-Trent contributed to the distinctive taste of the pale ales brewed there; the soft water in Pilzen, Czech Republic, was an important element of its acclaimed lagers. Now, scientific techniques enable brewers to alter tap water so that it possesses the qualities needed for whatever style they may be brewing.

Malt, which supplies the fermentable sugars that become the alcohol in beer, is made when kernels of grain (usually barley but sometimes wheat or rye) are steeped in water until they germinate; they are then dried, and roasted in kilns. During the process, insoluble starches are converted into the soluble starches and sugar essential to the brewing process. By using different strains of grain, and kilning at different and varying temperatures, different kinds of malt are produced, each kind helping to create a style of beer with a distinctive colour, flavour, and aroma. Some brewers replace a portion of the malts with such less expensive adjuncts as corn and rice, which also contain fermentable sugars.

Hops, the cone-shaped "flowers" of a vine related to cannabis, have lupulin glands, which contain alpha acids that produce a bitterness that balances the sweeter malt tastes in beer, often create citrusy or floral aromas and flavours, and act as preservatives. In fact, when the British shipped beer to colonial officials in India, they used heavy doses of hops to help it survive the long sea journey. With over a hundred varieties of hops available, it is not surprising that the various hop extracts, powders, pellets, and whole flowers used in brewers' recipes (usually at a ratio of one part to over thirty parts of malt) have been called the spices of brewing.

Yeasts, one-celled micro-organisms, are essential to the brewing of beer. Without them there would be no beer, just a flat, malt-flavoured, non-alcoholic beverage. Yeasts feed on the fermentable sugars derived from malt or adjuncts and produce alcohol and carbon dioxide as "waste materials." Medieval monks, who brewed what was to them liquid sustenance, referred to yeast as "Godisgood." Early brewers often depended on airborne, invisible strains of this divine gift to alight on their liquid and work its heavenly miracles. Yeast was first specifically identified in the seventeenth century, and in the nineteenth century, the research of French scientist Louis Pasteur made possible the isolation and development of over a hundred strains that are used in brewing. In addition to producing alcohol, each strain of yeast contributes a different flavour to beer.

As well as these four basics, brewers sometimes include such ingredients as spices, fruits or fruit extracts, honey, maple syrup, and even spruce needles or juniper berries. Called additives, and distinct from adjuncts, these items do not generally influence the alcohol content of beer, but contribute additional flavours to the basic ones created by the interactions of the water, malt, hops, and yeasts.

Brewing and Brewing Equipment

Brewing begins after the brewer chooses a specific recipe, gathers the appropriate ingredients, and, perhaps most important, makes sure that the brewing equipment is clean—very, very clean. Without completely sanitized equipment, the possibilities of creating bad, spoiled beer are increased greatly.

The first step is milling chunks of malt into grist, which is then deposited in a large metal vessel called a mash tun, where it is mixed with water that is heated to around sixty-five degrees Celsius. In the resulting "porridge" or mash, the malt's starches are converted into fermentable sugars. The mash is strained and the wort, the sugar water, is placed in a brew kettle, to be vigorously boiled for between one and two hours. This process sterilizes the liquid and helps prevent contamination. During the boil, hops are added. The boil completed, the hop residue is separated and the liquid passed through a heat exchange unit where it is quickly cooled.

At this point, the liquid is essentially malt- and hop-flavoured water. However, after it is transferred to a fermentation tank and yeast is added, the wort's transformation into beer begins. Within eight to ten hours, the process of fermination is underway. For ales, which are made with top-fermenting yeast, the temperature in the fermentation tank is kept between sixteen and twenty degrees Celsius; for lagers, which use bottom-fermenting yeast, the tanks are kept at nine degrees Celsius. After eight to ten days, the now-alcoholic beverage is transferred to conditioning or aging tanks to mature. Ales are conditioned for up to two weeks, lagers for six weeks or more. At this point, the beer is ready to be delivered from the tanks to taps in a brewpub, or to be packaged in kegs, bottles, or cans.

Packaging Beer

For centuries, people took a pitcher or small bucket to the local pub or tavern, where they had it filled with beer and returned home. Late in the nineteenth century, when glass became cheaper to manufacture, beer began to be bottled, and after the Second World War, tin and later aluminum cans became the preferred containers for beer.

When the microbrewing revolution began in the late 1970s, purists insisted that bottles were the only acceptable containers. Cans, they said, gave beer a funny taste, and, perhaps more important to them, they felt that aluminum containers promoted ungenteel connotations of big-bellied men chugging pale yellow, fizzy mainstream lagers as they sat on the hoods of their pickup trucks.

Over the past decade, however, attitudes to canned beer have changed. Many microbrewers have either switched from bottles to cans or have begun to package in both bottles and cans. Bottles are expensive to clean and to ship, and can easily break or chip. Lightweight cans cool more quickly and, because they are airtight and keep light out, ensure a fresher, unspoiled product. They are popular with hikers and picnickers as they are easy to carry to and from a recreational destination.

The major disadvantage for microbrewers is the fact that cans, which must be printed with the label for a specific product, have to be ordered in large quantities. Having made an investment in up to 100,000 cans, a brewer must commit to making a large volume in the style indicated on the label. Bottles permit the brewing of smaller quantities and different styles; all that is required is a different label on the bottle.

But if people still want beer fresh from the conditioning tanks, just the way their great-great-grandfathers got it, they may be able to head to a nearby microbrewery or brewpub. They won't have to bring a bucket or pitcher; they can just ask for a growler—a half-gallon, reusable, screw-top glass bottle—or a party pig—a heavy six-and-a-half litre plastic container that stands on four legs. With the growler, they just unscrew the cap; with the pig, they obey the instructions: "Push the snout and the beer comes out."

Beer is Surrounded by Enemies

Beer has many enemies. They aren't legions of keg-smashing temperance zealots; they're light, heat, air, and time. Exposure to light (especially fluorescent light and sunlight) will cause a beer to become light struck and give it a "skunky" flavour. Brown bottles or (better yet) cans keep the harmful rays away from the liquid. Of course, sun can also warm the beer and make it taste insipid. If it is shelved in non-refrigerated areas at retail outlets or at home, or if it undergoes a series of temperature changes on the way from the store to home, its flavour can be changed for the worse.

Fresh air may be good for people, but it isn't good for beer. When oxygen interacts with it, the result is a stale, cardboard-tasting beverage. If there's too much space between the cap and the liquid level of the bottle, or if the cap isn't fitted tightly, the enemy air may be working on the contents.

The final enemy of beer is time. With the exception of some high-alcohol beers like barley wine, beer has a fairly short lifespan. After three or four months of sitting in the refrigerator or on store shelves, beer should be retired and sent down the sink to its final rest. Check the best-before date on the label if there is one, and, if there isn't, check to see that no dust has gathered on the shoulders of the bottle or top of the can. A dusty beer is probably an old beer.

When you get home, put your beer quickly into the fridge (making sure that the light is out when the door closes!) and don't save it for a festive occasion that is too far in the future. Don't be fooled by those ads showing a clear-glassed, open bottle of beer that's been set on a table at the edge of a sunlit tropical sea. The weather may be great, but the beer probably isn't.

Enjoying Your Beer

Many people can remember mowing the lawn in the backyard or chopping firewood at the campground or cabin and opening a can of what has been called "lawnmower beer," the stuff that's priced way below the other beers, and chugging it back. It quenches the thirst and if it gets warm or is spilt, it doesn't matter, because it was really cheap to begin with. But to enjoy fully a well-brewed lager or ale, it shouldn't be grabbed ice cold from the refrigerator or the ice chest and gulped from the bottle or can. In the last two decades, aficionados have developed a series of steps for enjoying beer that are as intricate as those obsessed over by wine lovers.

First, pour the beer carefully into a very clean, non-chilled glass. An improperly washed glass may contain traces of soap or other residue that can alter the taste of your beer. Glasses chilled in the freezer compartment may have attracted condensed moisture and food odours, and when beer is poured into them, the chill may lower the temperature below the intended serving ranges (from two to five degrees Celsius for mainstream lagers to ten to twelve degrees for ales and porters). Here's a good rule of thumb: the lighter colour of the beer, the lower the serving temperature.

Different shapes of glasses have been developed to enhance the appearance, aroma, and taste of specific styles. For example, the thin, tapered pilsner glass helps to support the delicate head and to release the carbonation of lagers. The goblet, resting on a thick stem and base, maintains the rich head of stronger Belgian ales. The *weizen* glass, tapered gracefully inward from the base and then slightly outward, captures the aromas of wheat beers. A brandy snifter is just right for swirling, sniffing, and sipping such high-alcohol brews as barley wine.

There are two schools of thought on how to pour a glass of beer. However, both have the same goals: to avoid spillage, to create a head that's about an inch high, captures the beer's aromas, and is attractive to the eye, and to release the appropriate amount of carbonation. One school advocates pouring the beer into the middle of an upright glass, pausing as often as necessary to prevent the foam from overflowing. The other recommends initially pouring the beer into a tilted glass, then gradually raising the glass to a vertical position to complete the pour.

Once the pour is completed, it's time—not to start drinking but to admire the beer in the glass. Notice its colour, the texture of the head, and the bubbles coming from the bottom of the glass. Lift the glass to your nose and enjoy the subtle malt and hop aromas rising from the foam.

Now it's time for the first taste—the most important one because the palate loses some of its sensitivity with succeeding sips. Take a hearty, rather than a delicate, sip—not an Adam's-apple-wobbling, chug-a-lug, "gee, it's hot today" gulp, but enough so that the beer can slide over and along the sides of your tongue on its way to the back of your mouth. The first impressions may be of the malt flavours, usually sweet and, in the case of beers made with darker malts, the taste of coffee or chocolate. The bitterness of the hops usually comes later, counter-balancing the malt's sweetness and often contributing floral or fruity tastes. Depending on the types of hops, malts, and yeasts used, a range of delicate flavours contrasting and complementing each other can be enjoyed in a sip of beer. And if the beer has additives—fruit, spice, or other things nice—taste them as well. They should be delicate and suggestive, not overwhelming.

As your sip is working its way across your mouth, you'll also experience what the beer experts call mouth-feel, the beer's texture. It will range from thin to full-bodied, depending on the style, and may be more or less effervescent depending on the level of carbonation. Lagers, especially mainstream ones, tend to be thin and highly carbonated, the darker ales more robust and frequently not so highly carbonated. Important though it is, the first taste won't tell you everything about the beer you are drinking. With later sips, different characteristics will become evident.

Enjoy the full experience of the beer. And when you're finished, don't forget to wash and rinse the glass thoroughly. Remember, cleanliness may or may not be next to godliness, but full enjoyment of your next beer depends on it.

Beer Styles

One of the most exciting things about the microbrewing revolution has been the tremendous increase in the number of styles of beer available to lovers of ales and lagers. No longer is the choice limited to something referred to generically as "beer" or, slightly more specifically, as "lager" or "ale." Canadian and American microbrewers have created their own versions of dozens of styles that have their origins in beers from British, Belgian, and German traditions. Cervesaphiles (a big word for beer lovers) no longer have to purchase expensive brands from across the Atlantic Ocean. Now they can buy equally good and often better versions of the same styles from microbreweries that are frequently less than a two-hour drive from their own homes.

The characteristics of a given style of beer should not be considered a rigid set of specifications. Instead, they should be considered general traits—of ingredients, appearance, and taste—shared by a group of beers. For many consumers, one of the many joys of the microbrewing movement is the availability of several different versions of the same style, each one an embodiment of the brewer's creative interpretation.

The following guide to beer styles is divided into three sections: lagers, ales, and specialty beers. Within each category, styles are listed alphabetically. Following each description are some Alberta and British Columbia examples of the style. In putting together the style descriptions, I have drawn on several sources. Randy Mosher's *Tasting Beer: An Insider's Guide to the World's Greatest Drink* (Storey Publishing, 2009), Garrett Oliver's *The Brewmaster's Table* (HarperCollins, 2003) and Dan Rabin and Carl Forget's *The Dictionary of Beer and Brewing* (Brewers Publications, 1998) have very useful discussions. *All About Beer Magazine*, a bi-monthly publication, carries an article on a specific beer style in each issue. The Brewers Association website also has brief descriptions of each beer style: craftbeer.com/pages/style-finder.

Lagers

Lagers, which use bottom-fermenting yeasts, are generally more highly carbonated and lighter bodied than most ales. Since the development of refrigeration in the later part of the nineteenth century, lagers, which must be brewed and stored at lower temperatures, grew greatly in popularity, particularly in the United States. There, brewers from Germany, the birthplace of most lagers, created versions of the beers of their homeland and established very large breweries and extensive distribution networks. Lagers, particularly North American styles, have become the most widely consumed beers in the world.

Bock: this German-style beer has much fuller and robust flavours than other lagers. Lightly hopped, it is dark in colour—from copper to deep brown—and medium- to full-bodied.
Canoe Bavarian Copper Bock

Bohemian (Czech) Pilsner: a light-bodied, clear, light-straw-coloured to golden beer, with a crispness imparted by the hops. It was originally brewed in Pilsen, where the soft water enhanced the crisp cleanness of the beer.
Banff Ave Czuggers Pilsner, Big River Pilsner, Brewsters Czech Pilsner, Dockside Johnston Street Pilsner, Grizzly Paw Powder Hound Pilsner, Jasper Sutter Hill Pilsner, Phillips Phoenix Gold Lager, R&B Bohemian (Iceholes) Lager, Russell Extra Special Lager, Storm Precipitation Pilsner, Surgenor Steam Donkey Lager

Doppelbock: stronger in alcohol content and fuller bodied and darker coloured than *bock*, it often has chocolate and coffee tastes.
Phillips Instigator Doppelbock

Dunkel: light to dark brown in colour, this full-bodied lager has rich malty flavours.
Pacific Western Canterbury Dark Mild, Phillips Dr. Funk Dunkel, Vancouver Island Hermann's Dark Lager

Eisbock: a full-bodied, copper- to black-coloured beer in which part of the water content has been frozen and removed to increase the alcohol content to between 8 and 15 per cent ABV. The resulting beverage is malty in flavour and has little hop bitterness.
Vancouver Island Hermannator Ice Bock

German Pilsner: a light- to medium-bodied, straw- to gold-coloured lager that has spicy hop notes and a slight malt sweetness. It is fuller in body than Czech pilsners and somewhat maltier.

Central City Red Racer Lager, Pacific Western Pacific Pilsner, Old Yale Cultus Lake Pilsner, Russell Rocky Mountain Pilsner, Shuswap Lake Canoe Creek Pilsner

Helles: from the German word meaning "bright" or "pale," this medium-bodied beer balances malt and hop flavours. Light straw to golden in colour, it often features toasty malt flavours.

Alley Kat Charlie Flint's Lager, Craig Street Cowichan Bay Lager, Dockside Marina Light Lager, Lighthouse Fisgard 150 Lager, Lighthouse Lager, Okanagan Spring 1516 Bavarian Lager, Steamworks Lions Gate Lager, Swans Old Towne Bavarian Lager, Yellowhead Lager

Maibock: a gold-coloured *bock* available in the later spring (May). It is distinguished by the sweet malty notes and relatively light body.

Phillips Springbock

Marzen: full-bodied, very malty, copper-coloured beer with crisp hop bitterness.

Swans Lederhosen Lager

North American Lager: pale in colour, very light in body, and highly carbonated, with minimal hop and malt flavours. This is the most widely consumed style of beer in the world. Some brewers replace a portion of the malts with such cheaper adjuncts as corn and rice, further reducing the malt flavour.

Barley Mill Classic Draft Lager, Big Ridge Harvest Lager, Big Rock Gopher Lager, Bowen Island Lager, BrewHouse at Whistler Lifty Lager, Brewsters Original Lager, Budweiser, Cannery 360 Lager, Dead Frog Lager, Drummond Lager, Freddy's Brewpub/Mill Creek Brewery Back Country Lager, Granville Island Lager, Kokanee, Labatt Blue, Longwood Lulu's Lager, Molson Canadian, Okanagan Spring Hopped Lager, Okanagan Spring Premium Lager, Pacific Western Cariboo Genuine Draft, Pacific Western Natureland Lager, Red Truck Lager, Ridge Genuine Draft, Roughneck Pipeline Lager, Russell BC Lions Lager, Tree Beach Blonde Lager, Tree Kelowna Pilsner, Turning Point Hell's Gate Lager, Vancouver Islander Lager,

Whistler Powder Mountain Lager, Whistler Premium Export Lager, Yaletown Mainland Lager, Yukon Chilkoot Lager

North American Light Lager: a lower alcohol (usually around 4 per cent ABV) version of North American Lager. It is sometimes made by diluting regular-strength lager.

Barley Mill Caballero Cerveza Lager, Big Rock Jack Rabbit, Bowen Island Special Light, Bud Light, Coors Light, Kokanee Light, Pacific Western Traditional Light

Oktoberfest: a medium-bodied fall beer with smooth caramel malt flavours that are balanced with a hop bitterness.

Wild Rose Oktoberfest

Schwarzbier: from the German word for "black," this very dark beer is light- to medium-bodied. The roasted barley malts give chocolatey flavours that are balanced with low to medium hop bitterness.

Alley Kat Alligator Blackened Lager, Banff Ave Lower Bankhead, Brew Brothers Black Pilsner, Okanagan Spring Brewmaster's Black Lager, Surgenor #8 Shaft Black Lager

Steam Beer (also called California Common Beer): so called because of the hissing sound when a keg is tapped. Developed in California in the nineteenth century, this beer is amber-coloured, medium-bodied, and fairly highly hopped. Anchor Steam Brewing Company of California has copyrighted the term "steam beer."

Vienna Lager: medium-bodied and reddish-brown to copper in colour, this lager has a malt sweetness balanced with a clean, crisp, but not too strong, hop bitterness.

Big River Vienna Lager, Canoe Red Canoe Lager, Dockside Old Bridge Dark Lager

Ales

Until the later nineteenth century, when German-style lagers became extremely popular in the United States, ales were the most widely consumed beers in the world. Using top-fermenting yeasts, they do not require the cooler temperatures for fermenting and conditioning that lagers do, and the brewing cycles are much shorter. Generally speaking, ales are fuller bodied, darker in colour, and richer and more robust in flavour. When the microbrewing revolution began in the 1980s, most microbrewers produced ales, preferring to offer beers that were different in taste from those of the megabrewers. Often they went back to the ale traditions of the British Isles and Belgium (and, to a lesser extent, Germany) to create beverages that have appealed to a growing number of consumers.

Alt: from the German word meaning "old" (as in traditional), this copper- to brown-coloured ale has toasted malty flavours balanced by hop notes that help to create a clean, crisp finish.

Driftwood Crooked Coast Amber Ale, Gulf Islands Whaletail Ale, Vancouver Island Sea Dog Ale

Amber Ale: this copper to light-brown beer has been called "a darker pale ale." Fuller bodied than a pale ale, it is noted for its balance between caramel malt notes and citrusy hop flavours.

Alley Kat Amber Ale, Big Ridge Rodeo Red, Cannery Anarchist Amber Ale, Granville Island Gastown Amber Ale, Howe Sound Three Beavers Ale, Lighthouse Race Rocks Ale, Pacific Western Natureland Amber Ale, Phillips Blue Buck Ale, Red Truck Ale, Ridge Amberdillo, Tin Whistle Kettle Valley Amber Ale, Tree Thirsty Beaver Amber Ale, Turning Point Stanley Park 1897 Amber Ale

American Blonde Ale: lightly to moderately hopped, this straw-coloured to golden-blonde beer is light-bodied and crisp; it is often compared to lagers and offered as a crossover beer to people used to mainstream products.

Big River Blonde Ale, Gulf Islands Salt Spring Golden Ale, Longwood Blonde Ale, Mission Springs Bombshell Blonde Ale, Roughneck Driller's Ale, Shuswap Lake Station House Blonde Ale, Swans Arctic Ale, Tin Whistle Centennial Ale

American Wheat Ale: an American version of *hefeweizen* that is frequently filtered.

Barley Mill Cayuse Wheat Ale, Big Rock Grasshopper, Brewsters Wild West Wheat Ale, Wild Rose Velvet Fog, Wild Rose Wred Wheat Ale

Barley Wine: high in alcohol content (usually over 10 per cent ABV), this has been called a "sipping beer." It is full-bodied and dark brown in colour and has complex malt flavours that include caramel, toasty, and fruity notes.

Belgian Blonde Ale: light- to medium-bodied, gold to deep amber in colour, this ale has a malty sweetness, spicy notes, and moderate hoppiness.

Belgian India Pale Ale: *see India Pale Ale.*

Belgian Strong Dark Ale: strong in flavour, high in alcohol content, and full-bodied, it features chocolate, raisin, and caramel malt flavours, with notes of burnt sugar.

Bitter: the beer that is most often associated with an evening at an English pub, it has a balance between malt sweetness and hop bitterness, with earthy, nutty, and grainy flavours. Light-bodied and gold to copper in colour, this session beer is lower in carbonation and in alcohol content than many beers (usually under 5 per cent ABV). *See also Extra Special Bitter (ESB).*

Brown Ale: one of the most popular English styles, brown ale is noted for its rich malt flavours, including nutty, toffee, and chocolate notes. This medium-bodied beer is generally sweet, although moderate hopping prevents the sweetness from becoming overwhelming.

Appleton Brown, Tin Whistle Black Widow Brown Ale, Wild Rose Brown Ale, Yaletown Downtown Brown

Cream Ale: straw to pale gold in colour, this light-bodied ale is high in carbonation but low in hop bitterness and has a malty sweetness.

Big Rock Warthog Ale, Bowen Island Irish Cream Ale, Mission Springs Big Chief Cream Ale, Mt. Begbie Cream Ale, Phillips Slipstream Cream Ale, R&B Raven Cream Ale, Russell Cream Ale, Shaftebury Cream Ale

Dark Mild: a popular session beer that is light- to medium-bodied and gold to dark brown in colour. Fairly low in alcohol (usually under 5 per cent ABV) and in carbonation, it has almost no hop presence. Sweet chocolate and caramel malt flavours dominate.

Big Rock Traditional Ale, Nelson After Dark, Spinnakers Mt. Tolmie Dark, Whistler Black Tusk Ale

Dubbel: a Belgian ale noted for its rich malty flavours and spicy notes. Dark amber to brown, it is lightly hopped. Generally sweet, with a light to moderate bitterness, it has a dry finish.

Driftwood Brother Bart's Belgian Brown, Yaletown Jolly Hooligan

Dunkelweizen: a wheat beer that uses dark malts and is sweeter than *hefeweizen*.

Longwood Dunkel Weizen, Spinnakers Dark Wheat Beer

English India Pale Ale: *see India Pale Ale.*

English Pale Ale: *see Pale Ale.*

English Stout: *see Stout.*

Extra Special Bitter (ESB): a popular English-style beer, it is fuller bodied and higher in alcohol content than bitter. Although it has more bitterness than bitter does, rich malty flavours dominate. Dark gold to copper in colour, it is low in carbonation.

Banff Ave Brewer's Oar, Big River ESB, Canoe River Rock Bitter, Central City Red Racer ESB, Driftwood Naughty Hildegard Extra Special Bitter, Howe Sound Bailout Bitter, Howe Sound Baldwin and Cooper Best Bitter, Jasper Liftline, Longwood Extra Special Bitter, Plan B Bitter Bob Extra Special Bitter, Spinnakers John Mitchell's ESB, Swans Extra Special Bitter

Farmhouse Ale: *see* Saison.

Flanders *oud bruin*: this centuries-old Belgian style has recently become popular with beer aficionados. Light to medium in body and deep copper to brown in colour, it is both sweet and spicy. The use of burnt sugar contributes to the sweetness, while the yeasts and such additives as pepper provide spicy notes. It has a clean but sour finish.

Yaletown Oud Bruin

Fruit *Lambics*: *see* Lambic.

***Gueuze*:** *see* Lambic.

***Hefeweizen*:** from the German words for "yeast" and "wheat," this pale-to amber-coloured ale has been called "liquid bread," in part because the two ingredients noted in its name are principal ingredients in bread. Generally, close to 50 per cent of the malt used is wheat. Highly carbonated, it has virtually no hop character, but does have banana and clove notes. Because it is unfiltered, it has a hazy appearance.

Big Ridge Chimney Hill Wheat, Brewsters Gunther's Hefeweizen, Dockside Haupenthal's Hefeweizen, Granville Island Robson Street Hefeweizen, Nelson Liplock Summer Ale, Okanagan Spring Hefeweizen, Spinnakers Hefeweizen, Tree Hefeweizen, Whistler Weissbier, Yaletown Hill's Special Wheat

Imperial India Pale Ale: *see India Pale Ale.*

Imperial Stout: *see Stout.*

India Pale Ale (IPA): introduced in England in the late eighteenth century, this pale gold to amber ale is pale only in comparison to the darker ales that were popular at the time. It is more heavily hopped than pale ales. This high-hopping, which was originally meant to keep the beer from spoiling during the long, hot, sea journey to India, creates an intense bitterness. In English IPAs, the hop influence is moderated somewhat by the malts, which add bready and caramel notes. American West Coast IPAs, which have become very popular during the last two decades, are much more aggressively hopped. Not only does this increased hopping add to the bitterness, it also adds citrusy and floral tastes, and creates a very crisp, dry finish. Many American and Canadian microbrewers have created Double or Imperial IPAs, which are fuller bodied, intensely hoppy, and higher in alcohol content (from 7 to 10 per cent ABV). Belgian IPAs are noted for their bitterness, dryness, and high alcohol content.

Banff Ave Head Smashed IPA, Big Ridge Clover Ale, BrewHouse at

Whistler Dave's Dam Dangerous Drinkable IPA, BrewHouse at Whistler Woodward's IPA, Cannery India Pale Ale, Central City Red Racer IPA, Fat Cat Fat Head IPA, Granville Island Brockton IPA, Grizzly Paw Indra Island IPA, Howe Sound Devil's Elbow IPA, Howe Sound Total Eclipse of the Hop IPA, Jasper Rock Hopper IPA, Lighthouse Beacon IPA, Longwood IPA, Merecroft Village Railway IPA, Mission Springs Old Sailor IPA, Mt. Begbie Nasty Habit IPA, Nelson Paddywhack IPA, Old Yale Sergeant's IPA, Phillips Amnesiac Double IPA, Phillips Hop Circle IPA, Plan B Idiot Rock India Pale Ale, R&B Hoppelganger IPA, Ridge India Pale Ale, Roughneck Brewmaster's Choice India Pale Ale, Russell IP'eh!, Spinnakers Blue Bridge Double IPA, Spinnakers Fog Fighter (Belgian IPA), Spinnakers IPA, Steamworks Empress IPA, Storm Hurricane IPA, Swans Extra IPA, Taylor's Crossing Indian Arm IPA, Tree Hophead Double India Pale Ale, Tree Hophead India Pale,Wild Rose India Pale Ale, Yaletown Brick & Beam IPA

Irish Red Ale: a lightly hopped, medium-bodied, amber- to copper-coloured beer, with toasted malt notes and a caramel sweetness.

Big Rock McNally's Extra Irish Ale, Brewsters Hammer Head Red Ale, Brewsters Lanigan's Irish Ale, Craig Street Shawnigan Irish Red, Crannog Red Branch Irish Ale, Grizzly Paw Rutting Elk Red, Longwood Irish Red Ale, Spinnakers Roundhouse Red Ale, Surgenor Red House Ale, Yukon Red Ale

Irish Stout: *see Stout.*

Kolsch: originally brewed in Koln, Germany, this beer has been jokingly referred to as "the ale that wishes it were a lager," because of its light body, pale colour, and fairly high carbonation. It balances gentle hop and malt flavours, and has a crisp mouth-feel and a dry finish.

Banff Ave Blonde Ale, Mt. Begbie High Country Kolsch

Kristalweizen: a clear, filtered, straw-coloured to light amber version of *hefeweizen.*

Brew Brothers Tumbleweed Wheat, R&B Sun God Wheat Ale

Lambic: this four-hundred-year-old Belgian-style ale is unusual in that its fermentation process is natural or spontaneous, using wild yeast that is floating in the air. It has been described as fruity, earthy, sour or tart, and very dry. Gold to amber in colour, it is light-bodied and low in carbonation. Unmalted wheat is used in the brewing process.

Sometimes brewers will blend old (aged) *lambic* with young *lambic* to create *Gueuze,* a dry, fruity, effervescent beer. In Fruit *Lambics,* whole fruits are added after the start of fermentation and the resulting mixture is aged in oak or chestnut barrels. Kriek uses cherries, Framboise raspberries, Peche peaches, and Cassis black currants.

Spinnakers Currant Noir, Spinnakers Mon Cherie, Storm Blackberry Lambic, Storm Black Cherry Lambic, Storm Raspberry Lambic

Oatmeal Stout: *see Stout.*

Pale Ale: this gold to amber ale, which was much paler than the popular brown ales and porters of the late eighteenth century, balances nutty, caramel malt notes with a noticeable hop bitterness. English-style pale ale is more earthy in flavour than American West Coast-style pale ale, which has fuller hop bitterness, flavour, and aroma. Both are crisp and have a dry finish. Belgian pale ale is less bitter than the other two, is lighter bodied and has some malty sweetness.

Alley Kat Full Moon Pale Ale, Amber's Bub's Lunch Pail Ale, Barley Mill Pale Ale, Big River Pale Ale, Big Rock Pale Ale, Bowen Island Extra Pale Ale, Brew Brothers Ambush Pale Ale, Brewsters Rig Pig Pale Ale, Canoe Siren's Song Pale Ale, Cannery Pale Ale, Central City Red Racer Pale Ale, Craig Street Arbutus Pale Ale, Dead Frog Pale Ale, Dockside Cartwright Pale Ale, Driftwood Ale, Fernie The Grizz Pale Ale, Freddy's Brewpub/Mill Creek Brewery Lord Nelson's Pale Ale, Granville Island English Bay Pale Ale, Gulf Islands Salt Spring Pale Ale, Howe Sound Timberline Pale Ale, Lighthouse Riptide Pale Ale, Mt. Begbie Powerhouse Pale Ale, Nelson Old Brewery Pale Ale, Okanagan Spring Pale Ale, Old Yale Pale Ale, Plan B Revenge of the Pine Pale Ale, R&B Red Devil Pale Ale, Russell Pale Ale, Shuswap Lake Sam McGuire's Pale Ale, Spinnakers Ale, Steamworks Signature Pale Ale, Swans Pandora Pale Ale, Taylor's Crossing Two Lions Pale Ale, Tree Cutthroat Pale Ale, Turning Point Hell's Gate Pale Ale, Vancouver Island Piper's Pale Ale, Whistler Classic Pale Ale, Yaletown Nagila Pale Ale, Yukon Gold Ale

Porter: named after the late-eighteenth-century London workers for whom it was originally brewed, this brown to black, full-bodied ale uses several malts to create a complex variety of flavours. Relatively low in alcohol, it is moderately bitter.

Big Ridge Old Sullivan Porter, Craig Street Mt. Prevost Porter, Driftwood Blackstone Porter, Fat Cat Pompous Pompadour Porter, Gulf Islands Salt Spring Porter, Mt. Begbie Ol' Woodenhead Smoked Porter, Okanagan Spring Porter, Russell Black Death Porter, Steamworks Cole Porter, Tree Spy Porter

Roggen: this German ale uses malted rye and is both spicy and sour, with a noticeable hop finish.

Craig Street Rye Ale, Taylor's Crossing Roggen Weizen

Russian Imperial Stout: *see Stout.*

Saison **or Farmhouse Ale:** designed as a beer with which farm workers could quench their thirst during hot summer days in the fields, this Belgian-style ale is gold to amber in colour, light- to medium-bodied, and highly carbonated. It is spicy (often white pepper is used), moderately bitter, fruity, and sour or tart.

Driftwood Farmhand Ale

Scotch Ale or Wee Heavy: this strong, dark, creamy ale is full-bodied. Mahogany in colour, it has caramel flavours and sometimes, depending on the malt used, smoky notes.

Cannery Squire Scotch Ale, Phillips Double Barrel Scotch Ale, Russell Wee Angry Scotch Ale, Swans Riley's Scotch Ale

Scottish Ale: designated as light, heavy, or export depending on the alcohol content, this ale is not as strong as Scotch Ale. Malt flavours dominate over hops.

Spinnakers Jameson's Scottish Ale, Storm Highland Scottish Ale

Stout: originally called "stout porter" when it was first brewed early in the nineteenth century, stout is fuller bodied than porter. Dark brown to an opaque black, it is noted for the roasted flavours, imparted by the malted and unmalted barley. English stout is a somewhat sweet ale with caramel and chocolate flavours, which are balanced by the hop bitterness. Irish Stout is dryer than English versions and often has coffee and chocolate flavours. Designed to be a session beer, it is slightly lighter in body than English versions. Oatmeal Stout, in which unmalted oatmeal is added in the brewing process, is much smoother in texture than either the English or Irish versions. Russian (Imperial) Stout, which was originally brewed for Catherine the Great, has an alcohol content above 10 per cent ABV. It is not only more bitter than other stouts, it also has much fuller malt flavours. Amber's Kenmount Road Chocolate Stout, Banff Ave Reverend Rundle Stout, Big River Stout, Big Rock Black Amber Ale, BrewHouse at Whistler Black Diamond Stout, BrewHouse at Whistler Heart of Darkness Imperial Stout, Crannog Back Hand of God Stout, Grizzly Paw Moose Knuckle Oatmeal Stout, Howe Sound Diamond Head Oatmeal Stout, Howe Sound Pothole Filler Russian Imperial Stout, Jasper 6060 Stout, Lighthouse Keeper's Stout, Mission Springs Fat Guy Stout, Longwood Russian Imperial Stout, Mt. Begbie Selkirk Stout, Nelson Blackheart Oatmeal Stout, Old Yale Sasquatch Stout, Plan B McHugh's Oatmeal Stout, R&B Dark Star Oatmeal Stout, Spinnakers Oatmeal Stout, Steamworks Heroic Stout, Storm Black Plague Stout, Swans Oatmeal Stout, Taylor's Crossing Mad Scow Stout, Wild Rose Alberta Crude Oatmeal Stout, Yaletown Warehouse Stout

Tripel: Although lighter in body than *dubbel*, this Belgian ale is stronger—7 to 10 per cent ABV. Bright yellow to gold, it has spicy and fruity notes, and sweetness that is balanced by a moderate hop bitterness.

Central City Red Racer Belgian Tripel, Phillips Surly Blonde Big Belgian Tripel, Yaletown Le Nez Rouge

West Coast India Pale Ale: *see India Pale Ale.*

West Coast Pale Ale: *see Pale Ale.*

Witbier: from the Belgian word for "white," this unfiltered wheat beer is pale and cloudy because it is unfiltered. Highly carbonated and crisp, it is light- to medium-bodied and is often flavoured with coriander and orange peel.

Central City Red Racer Wheat Ale, Driftwood White Bark Wheat Ale, Fernie Ol' Willy Wit, Howe Sound Whitecap Wheat Ale, Shuswap Lake Talking Dog Wit, Steamworks Ipanema Summer White Ale, Swans Tessier's Witbier

Specialty Beers

In addition to creating a great variety of styles through their different uses of the four basic ingredients of beer—malt, hops, yeasts, and water—some brewers use such additives as fruits, vegetables, herbs, spices, honey, chocolate, and coffee to introduce nuances of flavour.

These additives, which are included at various stages of the brewing process, should enhance the overall taste by complementing or contrasting the basic flavours rather than overpowering them. In the following list, where the name of a beer does not indicate what additive is used, the additive is named in parentheses.

Fruit and Vegetable beers: (Note that Belgian fruit *lambics* are not included in this list.)

Alley Kat Aprikat (apricot), Alley Kat Brewberry Blueberry Ale, Alley Kat Pumpkin Pie Ale, Banff Ave Stubble Jumper Saskatoon Berry, Big Rock Lime, Brewsters Blackfoot Blueberry Ale, Brewsters River City Raspberry Ale, Cannery Apricot Wheat, Cannery Blackberry Porter, Canoe Black Cherry Porter, Fernie What the Huck (huckleberry), Crannog Hell's Kitchen Ale (potato), Crannog Pooka Cherry Ale, Dead Frog Pepper Lime Lager, Dockside Jamaican Lager (hibiscus), Driftwood Belle Royale Belgian Strong Cherry Ale, Grizzly Paw Beaver Tail Raspberry, Howe Sound Pumpkin Eater Imperial Ale, Jasper Blueberry Vanilla Ale, Longwood Framboise (raspberry), Northam Black Bear Ale (blackberry), Phillips Crooked Tooth Pumpkin Ale, Russell Lemon Ale, Russell Lime Lager, Swans Berry Ale (raspberry), Swans Coconut Porter, Tin Whistle Peach Cream Ale, Tin Whistle Chocolate Cherry Porter, Wild Rose Cherry Porter, Wild Rose Wraspberry, Yukon Cranberry Wheat Ale

Herb and Spice beers: Amber's Australian Mountain Pepper Berry Lager, Canoe Winter Gale IPA (cinnamon, nutmeg, ginger), Granville Island Ginger Beer, Gulf Islands Heatherdale Ale (heather), Nelson Harvest Moon Hemp Ale

Honey and other "Syrup" beers: Amber's Sap Vampire Maple Lager, Big Rock Honey Brown Lager, Bowen Island Honey Brown Lager, Cannery Maple Stout, Canoe Summer Honey Wheat Ale, Dead Frog Honey Brown Lager, Dockside Alder Bay Honey Lager, Fat Cat Honey Beer, Freddy's Brewpub/Mill Creek Brewery Honey Ridge Ale, Granville Island Cypress Honey Lager, Granville Island Kitsilano Maple Cream Ale, Grizzly Paw Grumpy Bear Honey Wheat Ale, Howe Sound Garibaldi Honey Pale Ale, Jasper Honey Bear Ale, Merecroft Village Maple Leaf Logger, Nelson Wild Honey

Ale, Pacific Western Cariboo Honey Lager, Ridge Honey Ale, Russell Honey Blonde Ale, Shaftebury Honey Pale Ale, Spinnakers Honey Pale Ale, Swans Smooth Sailing Honey Ale, Tin Whistle Killer Bee Dark Honey Ale, Vancouver Island Skyhopper Honey Brown Ale, Whistler Altitude Honey Lager, Yukon Birch Bear (birch sap), Yukon Discovery Ale (honey)

Chocolate and Coffee beers: (Note that while some malts can impart coffee and chocolate notes to a beer, only those beers that actually contain coffee and chocolate are included in this list.)

Canoe Habit Espresso Stout, Granville Island Lions Winter Ale (white chocolate), Granville Island Rogers' Chocolate Stout, Tin Whistle Chocolate Cherry Porter, Yukon Midnight Sun Espresso Stout

Index of Craft Beers and Breweries of Alberta and BC

NOTE: For beers with distinctive nicknames, the name is listed first followed by the brewery name in parentheses, eg. Alder Bay Honey Lager (Dockside). For beers only named by the style, the name of the brewery is listed followed by the style, eg. Alley Kat Amber Ale.

Jon C. **Stott** is an English professor emeritus from the University of Alberta. Occasionally after class, Jon hit the pub with his colleagues for a pint, and thus developed a love of quality beer. His other interests include writing about children's literature and sports. In 1973, he wrote the Western Hockey League's official twenty-fifth anniversary commemorative magazine, and he has since authored three books on minor-league sports, including *Hockey Night in Dixie* and *Ice Warriors*. He has four publications on the study of children's literature, and in 2010, he retold stories from many lands in the children's book *A Book of Tricksters*. Jon lives in Edmonton, Alberta.

Things change, people move—check online for *Beer Quest West* updates and news at beerquestwest.com.